Malcolm Hillier
The HERB GARDEN

A DK Publishing Book

Visit us on the World Wide Web at
http://www.dk.com

PROJECT EDITOR LESLEY MALKIN   PROJECT ART EDITOR COLIN WALTON
MANAGING EDITOR MARY-CLARE JERRAM   MANAGING ART EDITOR AMANDA LUNN
US EDITOR MARY SUTHERLAND   PRODUCTION ALISON JONES

First American edition, 1996
2 4 6 8 10 9 7 5 3 1
Published in the United States by DK Publishing, Inc. 95 Madison Avenue New York, New York 10016

Library of Congress Cataloging-in-Publication Data
Hillier, Malcolm.
    The herb garden / by Malcolm Hillier. — 1st American ed.
        p.   cm.   Includes index.
    ISBN 0–7849–1052–4
    1. Herb gardening.   2. Landscape gardening.   I. Title
SB351.H5H54   1996
712 —dc20   96–13752
                                                                                    CIP

Computer page makeup by Colin Walton, Great Britain • Text film output by The Right Type, Great Britain
Reproduced by Pica, Singapore • Printed and bound by Butler and Tanner, Great Britain

CONTENTS

INTRODUCTION

THE VARIED AND BEAUTIFUL WORLD that is the plant kingdom contains myriad herbal species. Sporting some of the most attractive of all flowers and leaves, many have the additional advantage of aroma or fragrance. Given their immense practical value as well, their place in the ornamental garden is both highly desirable and assured.

SWEET CICELY
Myrris odorata

What is an herb? Most of us instantly think of kitchen herbs, such as thyme and rosemary, traditionally employed to flavor a range of dishes. Yet a far broader definition applies – one that I prefer. Herbs are plants that we have used from the earliest times, not only to flavor food but also in medicine, to beautify the body, and for other varied domestic purposes. Many species are attractive too, making ornamental value in the garden yet another asset.

This book is about growing herbs to maximum decorative effect in your garden. The vast array of herbal flower and foliage shapes and textures, their

rainbow of colors, and their aromas and sweet scents appeal to many of the senses, making them perfect subjects to enhance our gardens.

A dramatic resurgence of interest in herbal plants is bringing even more species to our attention; many of these are already popular ornamental garden favorites. Today, we employ an ever-widening range of fresh herbs to create delicious aromatic dishes. To this end, their scope has broadened beyond the familiar, well-loved parsley and sage, to basil, tarragon, and oregano, and still farther to exotically fragrant bee balm, lemon grass, cilantro, and saffron.

Some well-known cure-alls can have surprising herbal origins – willow *Salix alba*, for example, contains salicylic acid, an original ingredient of aspirin. Ongoing research continues to uncover potential wonder drugs: St. John's wort, *Hypericum perforatum*, and purple coneflower, *Echinacea* species, stimulate the immune system and are being tested as an AIDS treatment.

Tempting as it can be to concoct our own herbal remedies, remember that some herbal plants are poisonous and many can cause allergic reactions, so always consult a qualified authority before you administer anything.

△ AUTUMN HIPS
Seeds, berries, and fruits hold centerstage in autumn. In the limelight here are the seeds of old man's beard and the hips of dog roses.

◁ BOLD AND TRUE
Purple coneflower, Echinacea purpurea, *is visually stunning, but also has medicinal qualities – it stimulates the immune system.*

△ VELVETY SURPRISE

The velvety flamelike clusters of sumac, Rhus typhina, *persist long after the leaves have colored and dropped, making this a showy addition to the garden all year round.*

OLD-FASHIONED MIX ▷

Roses, catmint, and foxgloves overlap in their early to midsummer seasons to make a beauteous mix. Their uses are diverse, and their appearance always pleases.

△ FENNEL AND FRUIT

The feathery leaves of fennel form a delightful foreground to shiny, round crabapples on the tree behind. Both are useful in the kitchen too.

YEAR-ROUND BEAUTY ▷

Mahonia japonica *is a grand architectural shrub with attractive but vicious evergreen leaf fronds and scented yellow winter flowers.*

My Classic Herb Garden

SHOWN IN SUMMER, my dream herb garden combines formality and informality. Attractive paths provide access and lead to a central focal point, while the bench invites you to stay and savor the herbs around you. (For the detailed planting list see p.116.)

RUGOSA ROSE HEDGE •
An infomal hedge of roses supplies a long succession of highly scented flowers as well as vitamin C-packed hips.

MAGNIFICENT SHADES OF BLUE •
The beautiful blue flowers of chicory, borage, and nearby lavender make this a serene corner of the garden.

SPLASH OF GREEN FOR WINTER •
Evergreen juniper grows into a large shrub, the wiry shape giving it a wild air. It provides color in winter when other plants are drab.

STONE PATH WITH HERBS •
The gaps between uneven stone slabs play host to low, spreading herbs such as thyme and oregano.

CONTRASTING PAVING •
A combination of hard surfaces, in this garden stone flags, bricks, and gravel, offers interesting contrasts.

FORMAL TOPIARY SHAPES •
Juxtapose the neat formality of clipped boxwood pyramids with the informality of most other shrub and perennial herbs.

LOW, PERFUMED HEDGE •
Lavender can form a wonderfully loose evergreen hedge. Clip it back hard in spring to prevent it from becoming straggly.

BEE BALM
The many varieties of bee balm, Monarda didyma, *have fragrant leaves and beautiful flowers. I've planted them near the bench to enjoy their qualities to the full.*

SAFFRON CROCUS
Crocus sativus *only flowers with plenty of sun. It brings a welcome splash of color in the autumn, once its neighboring chives have finally ceased to produce flowers.*

N

SOMEWHERE TO RELAX
The perfect herb garden always has a comfortable • seat for contemplation.

DAPPLED SHADE
The light, delicate foliage of a birch tree casts a dappled shade in which herbs such as mints and • foxgloves thrive.

TALL REAR WALL
The sheltered face of a sunny brick wall provides the perfect place for growing • tender herbs.

• **ROSE HEDGE**
For a healthy floriferous hedge, choose from the many forms of rugosas available.

• **HARDWEARING PATH**
A herringbone (seen here), basket weave, or straight-running pattern of bricks is ideal for hardwearing paths. Leave spaces between the bricks to plant low herbs.

• **FRAGRANT ARCH**
Create a fragrant walkway with an arch of wood or metal supporting climbing and scented herbs such as roses, honeysuckle, jasmine, or hops.

• **NEAT WHITE PICKET FENCE**
A wooden picket fence forms an orderly boundary, without concealing the attractive plants growing behind it.

SILVER BIRCH TREE
Betula pendula *has a tracery of deciduous leaves that provides gentle shade for herbs preferring less intense sunlight, such as apple mint and foxglove.*

How to Plan your Garden

HERE ARE THE SIMPLE GUIDELINES that I follow when planning
an herb garden, redesigning an existing area or border, or just
adding new plantings. I always make a careful note of existing or
unchangeable features before starting to work out any additions
and changes, all with the help of a simple plan sketched to scale.

I find that it is much better, as far as is possible, to work with what you have, rather than attempting to change it. Happily, herbs to suit every site and situation abound.

First, you need to assess your soil pH and structure. To determine pH, do a few tests in different parts of the garden (you can buy a simple tester from a garden center). Soil structure ranges from heavy clay, through rich loam (ideal), to light and sandy. This influences its ability to drain. You can alter the structure a little by digging, either to lighten or to add body. If you wish to grow an herb that is entirely unsuited to your soil, containers with the appropriate potting mix present a practical and attractive solution.

Next, consider the nature of your site. Note where the main areas of shade are throughout the day and in the different seasons. Remember that there is more light under deciduous trees in winter. Also determine the local conditions in your garden: find the warm, sheltered sun-traps and the exposed or cold sites.

DRAWING A PLAN

When making large planting changes or alterations to the design of your garden, it is an enormous aid to be able to see a plan before committing to the work on site. Two people make light work of measuring up the boundaries

FIXED CONSIDERATIONS

Assess the elements and features you can't change before starting to make any alterations in your garden.

❧ SOIL TYPE The texture of your soil may be sandy, crumbly, stony, or sticky. It can be altered a little, but not much.
❧ SOIL pH Check the soil pH to see whether it is acid, neutral, or alkaline. Make your plant choice accordingly.
❧ MOISTURE Your soil may be dry and free-draining, waterlogged and sticky, or anywhere in between. The extremes can be improved, but it is wise to grow plants suited to existing conditions.
❧ ASPECT Monitor the progression of the sun to see how walls, fences, and trees affect light levels in your garden at different times of day.
❧ WHAT PLANTS? Find out a plant's hardiness, light, and soil requirements from your garden center to guarantee the right choice for your site. Other details, such as vigor and eventual size, whether it is deciduous or evergreen, and flower color, are also important.

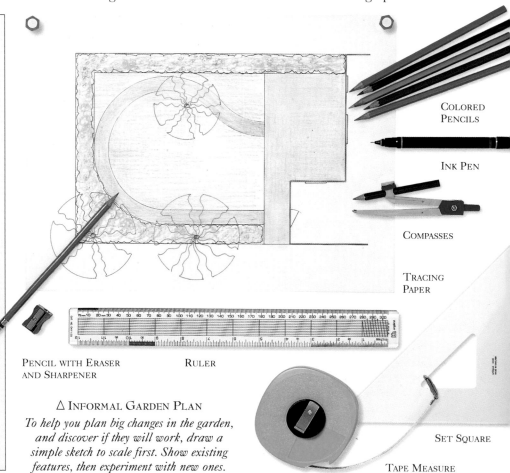

COLORED PENCILS

INK PEN

COMPASSES

TRACING PAPER

PENCIL WITH ERASER AND SHARPENER

RULER

SET SQUARE

TAPE MEASURE

△ INFORMAL GARDEN PLAN
To help you plan big changes in the garden, and discover if they will work, draw a simple sketch to scale first. Show existing features, then experiment with new ones.

of your garden. Once you have these measurements, scale them down and transfer to a sheet of tracing paper. Next, mark the main existing elements of the garden: paths, borders, paved areas, and features such as sundials or large statues. On the plan, show the growing point of hedges, trees, and sizeable shrubs. Measure the area each covers, reduce it to scale, and sketch it in. Now you can easily draft over-tracings to illustrate the new design features you want to incorporate. Always make these new features strong because the structure of a garden works best when it has an inner strength of definite curves and strong right angles – the planting can soften the lines later. Draw in pencil so you can make changes with ease.

With the attributes and limitations of the site clear in your mind, choose plants that will thrive where you grow them. Remember that plants must be seriously deterred not to thrive, for inherent in their nature is a desire to survive and grow well.

△ RUSTIC DECAY
Silvery purple sages pick up the stone and wood colors of an old greenhouse, adding a weathered and rustic feel to this garden.

HERB PARTERRE ▷
A formal parterre bed is solidly planted with silver-blue rue, edged by boxwood, and has a boxwood pyramid in the center.

△ INFORMAL HERB GARDEN
Herbs lend themselves well to both formality and informality; the mixture of a strong design shape with informal planting is my ideal. Here, the form of the herb garden is defined by the paving and hedges, but in the beds the herbs run riot. The planting softens and romanticizes the hard lines of paths and beds, while they contain the wilderness within.

YOUR CONSIDERATIONS

Before you spend money, time, and effort on your garden, give some thought to your requirements.

———— ✸ ————

❦ WHAT FOR? You may wish to grow herbs for a specific purpose, perhaps for their culinary, medicinal, or ornamental value, for scent, or for a combination of all these. Decide which are important to you and choose plants accordingly.

❦ WHO FOR? Consider the priorities, needs, and limitations of the people who will spend time in the garden. If you have children, for example, include play areas and grow poisonous plants out of reach; avoid steps for the elderly.

❦ STYLE OF GARDEN Decide if you want a formal or informal layout, or perhaps a combination of the two. Plan features such as paths, seating areas, and ponds, which reinforce your chosen style, and select herbs that will complement it.

❦ MAINTENANCE Consider how much work you are willing to do in the garden. Raised beds are accessible and simple to maintain; lawns are demanding.

Color Schemes

THE INSIGNIFICANT FLOWERS of a few herbs lead some of us to assume that herb gardens are not colorful. I have found, however, that striking foliage plus the showy flowers of a substantial number make it possible to create an enchanting range of themes in all colors.

I consider color in terms of temperature: red, yellow, orange, and purple are warm, while violet, green, and blue are cool. It follows that a yellow, orange, and red planting will look hot and sunny, but a violet, blue, and blue-green one will create a distant, cool, and serene effect. Colors close to each other on the color wheel, for instance, yellow and orange, or purple and violet, are easy on the eye. By contrast, "opposites" such as orange and blue or yellow and violet tend to be vibrant and exciting. Green – lovely in shades from silver- and golden green through pale and mid-greens to rich dark green – is ever-present in gardens, and works well with almost any effect.

Delicate pastels are uplifting and always attractive in groups – picture a swath of pale pink roses mixed with silver-leaved lavender and santolinas. Darker hues such as maroon, mustard, and dark green are more mysterious, regal, and brooding – think of prince's feather and many chrysanthemums.

Before committing to a scheme, experiment by scattering leaves and petals in your chosen colors. Vary the levels of light and background, which can alter the overall effect. Watch for color combinations that attract you in other gardens, and remember that colors are affected and offset by the shades that surround them. Create the moods that suit you and your garden by using varied colors in conjunction with herbal scents, textures, and forms.

△ BLUE AND SILVER ALL IN ONE

Even in one plant we can find a fascinating color mix. Above the intensely silver leaves, the blue of this sea holly's flowers carries into its bracts and stems. The mix is one we could continue into surrounding plants with bell flowers in front and globe artichokes behind.

◁ HARMONY OF YELLOW AND GREEN

Lying close to one another in the color wheel, yellow and green make good companions. Their mood is fresh, bright, and always sunny. Curry plant, with its rosemary-like leaves and gold flowers, forms an intricate tapestry with golden hops, fennel, and lemon balm.

△ HOT COLOR COMBINATION

*Pokeweed, with pale green leaves and berries
ripening to black on pinkish stalks, stands out
against firethorn's leaves and scarlet berries.*

◁ CLOSE COMPANIONS

*The dusky pink globes of these alliums combine
comfortably with the purple lavender. Both
are set off by the yew hedge in the background.*

▽ QUIRKY OPPOSITES

*In the striking combination of intensely silver
lavender cotton and rusty plum-colored
barberry, each plant lends interest to the other.*

Textures & Shapes

THE FORMS, SHAPES, AND TEXTURES of plants and their individual parts excite the eye and combine with color to make a garden interesting and unique. Herbs offer an engaging mix, an asset we can capitalize on when planning an entire garden or just a border or planting.

Texture, shape, and form are to some extent bound up with distance. I like to think of borders and flower beds in terms of the shapes of a larger landscape: mountains in the background perhaps, fronted by lower hills and valleys. We can emulate this profile in our gardens by growing larger shrubs and, perhaps, trees toward the back, then making mounds and valleys with groups of plants in front, using vertical spires of flowers to break their smooth outlines. Choose lower-growing herbs such as thyme or parsley to spill onto the grass or paving at the front.

In gardens, the shapes and outlines of every plant are plain to see, but the textures of their stems, leaves, and flowers are much better explored by coming close to examine and touch them. By choosing herbs that contrast with one another in texture you can cultivate intriguing relationships in your garden landscape. Play off smooth surfaces against jagged or prickly ones; fine, delicate leaves against large ones; matte against shiny. Contrast feathered rosemary or juniper shoots with the more rounded leaves and golden fruits of quince, or the sparse winter-tasseled twigs of alder with the close-knit, dark green foliage of a yew hedge. Play with height too: position large peony or rose heads to rise above a low frothy edging plant such as lady's mantle.

Make a note of combinations that attract you, then adapt them to create innovative plantings of your own.

△ DIFFERENT LEAF SHAPES

Although the huge fernlike leaves of artichoke, Cynara scolymus, *are many times larger than the tiny, spiky, aromatic gray leaves of lavender growing nearby, each has a beauty of its own. Contrasting them serves to heighten rather than detract from this beauty.*

◁ DRAMATIC CONTRAST

The seed heads and flower heads of these two plants could hardly be more different. Stately, but viciously barbed, the seed heads of teasle, Dipsacus fullonum *'Sativus', stand out dramatically against the billowing flower clouds of smoke tree,* Cotinus coggygria.

△ SOLID MEETS FEATHERY

The tiny aromatic leaves of tarragon are
arranged upward on their stalks. Their shape
echoes the beautiful veining in the large fleshier
leaves of horseradish plants in front of it.

FORM AND VARIEGATION ▷

Fortunately, the variegated form of ground
elder is not as rampant as its green parent. Its
lovely cream-splashed leaves make a striking
contrast to the spears of variegated sedge.

△ LOLLYPOP FLOWERS

A thicket of Chinese chives takes center stage in
front of feathered rosemary. The upright chive
stalks are crowned by round spangled heads
of long-lasting tubular white flowers.

◁ VARYING SCALE

Mullein's large silvery leaves, arranged in a
rosette, are similar in shape to those of
Jerusalem sage, but their vast difference in
size makes them interesting bedfellows.

Herb Garden Features

BORDERS & FLOWER BEDS

IT IS IN THE BORDERS, up the walls and fences that stand behind them, and in our flower beds where we can grow the widest range of herbs, from tall ones at the back down to small edging plants in front, with everything to choose in between. Use shrubs and small trees to form a framework and a selection of perennial and annual herbs within it.

Borders are the mainstay of almost all gardens, and, as such, should be filled with exciting combinations of colors, textures, forms, and perfumes. A surprising number of herbs are ideal for borders and training up the walls behind them; your problem is more likely to be a choice of far too many enticing plants and not enough room to grow them all.

Introduce a strong structure of evergreen herbs to provide winter interest as well as attraction in summer. Bay, boxwood, broom, cistus, lavender cotton, laurel, lavender, mahonia, rosemary, and many more put on a decorative foliage display throughout the year. Remember to consider the eventual height and spread of each plant when making your choice.

I like borders and beds to appear opulent, showing little soil from early summer to autumn. To achieve this, fill in the evergreen framework with a multitude of deciduous perennials and shrubs, leaving pockets for special annuals such as nasturtiums, poppies, love-in-a-mist, and marigolds. Onions, crocuses, and lilies are among herbal bulbs that earn a place in any border.

Cultivate tender climbers and wall shrubs such as jasmine, confederate jasmine, and passion vine against sunny walls or fences, if you have them, since this protects them from the elements. Less tender, but happiest in sun, are the many beautiful climbing roses. Choose ivies, honeysuckle, and hops for bright but shaded spots.

△ CLOAK OF CATMINT
Catmint is wonderfully aromatic, and much enjoyed by cats and other passers-by. This low wall shows off its purple flowers beautifully.

◁ SWEET EXCESS OF SUMMER
A wide border backed by a brick wall forms a perfect sun-trap for, among others, evening primrose, an apothecary's rose, and chicory.

PASTORAL PASTELS ▷
In a bulging border backed by a wall, the soft colors of roses, geranium, foxgloves, feverfew, and calamint are offset by mixed green foliage.

A Tracery of Twigs

WHEN PLANTS ARE COVERED in lush green leaves it is easy to forget how beautiful many of their bare branches and twigs can be in the winter months, particularly when seen against a clear blue sky. Add fruits, catkins, and a smattering of scented flowers for a wondrous winter tracery that is quite as beautiful as any summer display.

POLLARDED WILLOWS

The white willow, here in its red growth form, Salix alba vitellina *'Britzensis', is of great medicinal value; it contains salicylic acid, used in the preparation of aspirin. It also helps to soothe sore throats.*

HOARY HAWTHORN

Hawthorn, Crataegus laevigata, *is beautiful in borders – its spring flowers are a delight and from autumn into winter, the scarlet haws are decorative. All parts treat heart problems and regulate blood pressure.*

Gardener's Notes

This striking winter group for the woodland garden enjoys a moist spot. Alders are extremely attractive in winter, first with black fruits, followed by the catkins seen here. Pussy willow seems to spell out the end of winter; some northern countries use it instead of palms on Palm Sunday. The contorted shapes of tortured willow are impressive in winter when at their most obvious, and witch hazel's strange, spidery flowers are deliciously perfumed.

❦ SITE & SOIL Plant in moisture-retentive soil in a sunny or semishaded position. Willows are attractive associated with water; grow willows and alders only if the ground is sufficiently moist or they are close to a pool.

❦ PLANT CARE Cut pussy willows and pollarded white willows back in early spring to encourage new growth for the following winter.

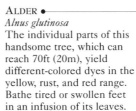

ALDER ●
Alnus glutinosa
The individual parts of this handsome tree, which can reach 70ft (20m), yield different-colored dyes in the yellow, rust, and red range. Bathe tired or swollen feet in an infusion of its leaves.

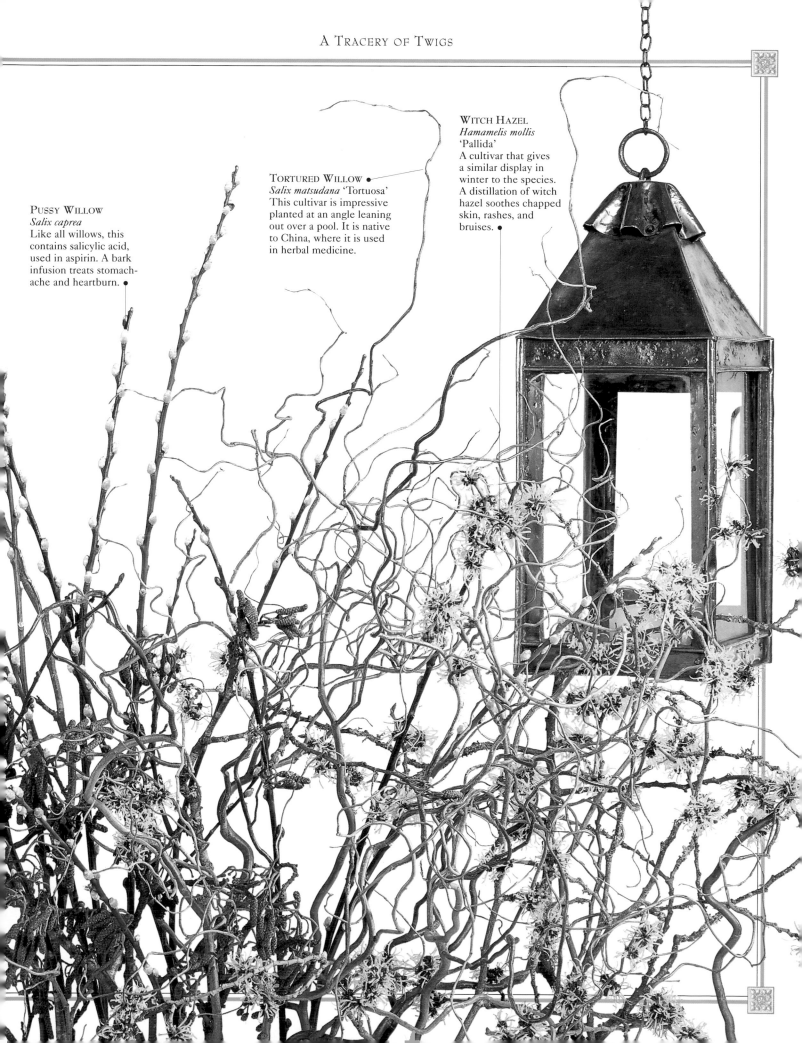

WITCH HAZEL
Hamamelis mollis
'Pallida'
A cultivar that gives
a similar display in
winter to the species.
A distillation of witch
hazel soothes chapped
skin, rashes, and
bruises.

TORTURED WILLOW •
Salix matsudana 'Tortuosa'
This cultivar is impressive
planted at an angle leaning
out over a pool. It is native
to China, where it is used
in herbal medicine.

PUSSY WILLOW
Salix caprea
Like all willows, this
contains salicylic acid,
used in aspirin. A bark
infusion treats stomach-
ache and heartburn. •

Spring Song

IT IS ALWAYS EXCITING to see the first chorus of flowers heralding the coming of spring. Of the herbal plants, primroses and sweet violets are early to flower. A little later come cowslips, bluebells, and the pretty golden flower heads of alexanders. Relish these herbal treasures; they are among relatively few to emerge in early spring.

ALEXANDERS

The tall umbels of golden flowers belong to alexanders, Smyrnium olusatrum, *also known as black lovage. Its stems and flowers can be used in the same way as celery, as a flavoring for soups and salads.*

GREEN-GOLD HERALD OF SPRING

Large numbers of honey-scented cowslips, Primula veris, *used to grow wild. Now protected, we must rely on homegrown plants for cowslip wine. Here they nestle beneath* Philadelphus coronarius *'Aureus'.*

NATURALIZED BLUEBELLS

A swath of bluebells, Hyacinthoides non-scripta, *growing wild in the dappled shade of brilliant new pea-green leaves is arguably the most wonderful sight of the season. Bluebell bulbs are very rich in starch.*

WHITE CEDAR •
Thuja occidentalis
'Rheingold'
An extract from the
extremely aromatic
leaves combats bronchial
and urinary infections,
and its twigs are used
to treat rheumatism.

WESTERN RED CEDAR •
Thuja plicata 'Zebrina'
The variegated fronds of this
conifer are grapefruit-scented.
As with white cedar above, the
leaves are given for coughs and
also to treat urinary infections.

Gardener's Notes

Despite their diminutive stature, the violets
have a perfume that carries well. So, too, do
many primroses, especially the bright colored
flowers of the polyanthus group. The conifers
are heady with citrus notes, making this an
astoundingly perfumed spring group.

❧ SITE & SOIL Primroses and violets like to
nestle at the base of a hedge or on a bank, but
must be moist at the roots. Conifers take up a
great deal of moisture, so instead of planting
primroses and violets nearby in the ground,
consider growing them in pots, where they will
thrive in dappled shade. Conifers prefer sun.

❧ PLANT CARE Make sure that the ground does
not dry out too much in winter, but do not
water when the soil is frozen. Watch out for
slug damage on the primroses and violets.

• **SWEET VIOLET**
Viola odorata
Crystallize the flowers
for decoration on cakes
and desserts. An extract
from both leaves and
flowers treats respiratory
problems. The oil is
used in perfumery.

PRIMROSE •
Primula vulgaris Polyanthus Group
Like those of violets, the flowers
can be crystallized. They and the
baby leaves are added to salads. A
root decoction is a cough remedy.

Breath of Spring

As THE DAYS BEGIN to lengthen, a succession of beauties display their attributes. The hazel catkins emerge early, their tiny flowers dusting the cool air with pollen. Witch hazels scent the air on sunny days, while in warmer areas sunshine baubles of mimosa preempt almond blossoms.

MIMOSA
Acacia falciformis
Flowers, seeds, and shoots of acacias are edible. The plants tolerate dry soil and improve its fertility. An infusion alleviates diarrhea and externally treats skin complaints.

SCENT OF APPLES

The soft white-flushed pink apple blossom of Malus 'Bolero' *has a special perfume that is essence of spring. When tasting its sugared petals on cakes and desserts, you shouldn't regret having sacrificed the fruit.*

WITCH HAZELS FOR FRAGRANCE

The many forms of Hamamelis x intermedia, *here 'Jelena', have the best scent of all witch hazels. Leaves and stems of H. virginiana are used commercially to make the distillation that treats cuts and bruises.*

Gardener's Notes

SNOW GUM
Eucalyptus pauciflora
subsp. *niphophila*
The camphor-scented oil
of eucalyptus makes an
excellent decongestant,
helpful in the relief of
bronchitis. It can also be
applied externally to
bruises and wounds. •

This group of trees offers color, form, and texture to ease
us through winter into spring. They range from 30ft (7m)
to 40ft (12m) in height. Snow gum has large, pointed
adult leaves, and is not as fast-growing as other trees
in the genus. Hazel produces its nuts in autumn.
❦ SITE & SOIL Hazel likes semishade; the others, sun.
All need well-drained soil. Avoid cold, exposed sites.
❦ PLANT CARE Hazelnuts are produced on the
previous year's new growth, so
prune with care. Plant eucalyptus
as seed or very small plants to
help them develop strong
roots early on.

ALMOND
Prunus dulcis
Seeds are added to sweet and
savory dishes, particularly in
Middle Eastern recipes.
Almond oil is used in many
• commercial cosmetics.

• HAZEL CATKINS
Corylus avellana
Add the oil to salad
dressings and the nuts
to both savory and
sweet dishes. The
twigs are traditionally
used for water divining.

Perfumed Wall

MANY CLIMBING PLANTS, shrubs, and tall perennials enjoy growing
in a border against a wall. Several have well-scented flowers. Here
I have narrowed the choice down even more to herbs that also have
white flowers, and again, there are plenty of these. Most thrive in
a sunny position where the warmth of a wall offers protection.

ENCHANTED EVENING
The drooping trumpets of flowering tobacco, Nicotiana sylvestris, *have
a sweet nutmeglike perfume, particularly intense in the evening. The
leaves contain nicotine, which can be used as an insecticide.*

VARIEGATED ELDER
Sambucus nigra 'Marginata'
All forms of *S. nigra* may
be used medicinally to
treat colds, as well as
rheumatism and arthritis.

STAR-COVERED CLOAK
Confederate jasmine, Trachelospermum jasminoides, *with a cascade
of highly perfumed flowers continuing throughout the summer, is
a popular evergreen. In Eastern medicine it treats arthritis.*

Gardener's Notes

This highly perfumed group of tall shrubs and trees is beautiful against a boundary, where it may be fronted by white roses, lavenders, and tobacco plants. Mock orange has an incredibly intense scent, as do elder flowers and privet. I relish their heady fragrances, although some may find the combination a little too powerful.

❧ SITE & SOIL These are easy to grow in any garden soil, preferably in a reasonably sunny place. A wall behind offsets them perfectly.

❧ PLANT CARE Cut back straggly old growth on deciduous mock orange after flowering. Semi-evergreen privet clips well into hedges or shapes once new growth has hardened. Prune the old growth of deciduous elder in winter.

GOLD-LEAVED ELDER
Sambucus nigra 'Aurea'
Use the flowers of all elders to flavor cordials or stewed fruits such as gooseberries, apples, and rhubarb. ●

MOCK ORANGE
Philadelphus 'Belle Etoile'
The flowers have a unique sweet lemony fragrance, used in potpourri and perfume. ●

PRIVET
Ligustrum vulgare
The flowers are made into eau de toilette, and an infusion soothes sunburn. *L. lucidum* is a close relative that treats respiratory diseases and strengthens the
● immune system.

BRONZE ELDER
Sambucus nigra
'Guincho Purple'
The berries of elders can be used like currants in tarts and pies, and add color and
● flavor to wines and port.

Early Summer Scents

SWEET OR AROMATIC, herb perfumes are at their most intense in early summer. The first roses, especially the damasks and gallicas, and peonies such as 'Kelway's Supreme' and 'Laura Dessert', pour forth their fruit-sweet scents, while all around you can introduce the leafy aromas of sage, lavender, and rosemary.

PEONY
Paeonia 'Bunker Hill'
The roots, flowers, and seeds of peonies can help blood and circulation problems. *P. suffruticosa* treats eczema in children.

ALLIUM
Allium sphaerocephalon
This attractive plant has the distinct onion scent when bruised. Its flowers can be used in salads. All alliums purify the blood and reduce blood pressure.

ROSEMARY
Rosmarinus officinalis
As suggested in Hamlet –
"There's rosemary, that's for remembrance" – this herb was once thought to quicken the memory.

Gardener's Notes

An enchanting group for the early summer border, this has interesting flower and leaf, color, form, and texture combinations. Many peonies have a delicious rosy scent, which here mixes well with the fragrant leaves of both rosemary and Jerusalem sage. Even the allium flowers are sweetly scented, although they smell oniony when bruised or cut.

❧ SITE & SOIL Grow in a sunny position in rich, well-drained soil. Peonies do not like acid soil.

❧ PLANT CARE Cut back any straggly growth on rosemary in spring, and Jerusalem sage after it has flowered. Peonies may need staking.

• JERUSALEM SAGE
Phlomis fruticosa
The sweetly aromatic leaves are used in Greece to make a soothing tea and may be added to potpourri.

CLASH OF HUES
The flowers of Rosa gallica *var.* officinalis *are the epitome of all roses. Here their color clashes excitingly with the pot marigolds, growing beside variegated germander,* Teucrium chamaedrys *'Variegatum'.*

ESSENCE OF SUMMER
The beautiful, highly perfumed flowers of Rosa *'Madame Isaac Pereire' mingle with aromatic pink Jerusalem sage, edible-flowered* Geranium pratense, *and gum cistus,* Cistus ladanifer, *with lovely white flowers.*

Cool Serenity

WHITE, THE COLOR OF LIGHT, appears in the flowers of many herbs.
Its cool but luminous quality can brighten whole areas of borders or
provide shining spotlights. From a froth of cow parsley to the huge
trumpets of lilies, white-flowered herbs produce a big impact.
Always serene, they have a wonderfully relaxing effect.

MAJESTIC BORAGE

*A bold but graceful white-flowered borage raises its stately head above
variegated lemon balm. Fronds of tarragon,* Artemisia dracunculus,
straggle through both plants to complete this foliage tapestry.

SHADES OF EARLY SUMMER

In the past, the decorative masterwort, Astrantia major, *was taken for
fevers, and wormwood,* Artemisia absinthium, *here in its beautiful
form 'Lambrook Silver', was used in the now-illegal absinthe liqueur.*

VIGOROUS COMPANIONS

The bright flowers of feverfew, Tanacetum parthenium, *bring constant
sunshine to the garden. Beautiful as an edging or in controlled clumps,
here they contrast with the sticky leaves of rock rose,* Cistus x aguilarii.

PURE WHITE

The white of Rosa rugosa *'Schneezwerg' is exceedingly pure, and its
scarlet autumn hips are most striking. Here it rises above ginger mint,*
Mentha x gracilis *'Variegata', which has lightly ginger-scented leaves.*

● FOXGLOVES
Digitalis purpurea f. *alba*
The leaves are highly toxic
but contain compounds
that are most effective
in the treatment of
heart disease.

MADONNA LILY
Lilium candidum
Deliciously sweet-
scented flowers are
used in perfumes,
and mucilage in the
bulb has a soothing
effect on certain
skin complaints. ●

Gardener's Notes

Tall foxglove spires, excellent planted at the
back of a border, and the many-headed stems
of the Madonna lily are bordered by lime-green
lady's mantle and sunny-centered feverfew in
this summer planting. Notice how the cool,
luminous whites are strengthened by their
association with bright lime-green and yellow.
❦ SITE & SOIL Grow in any reasonably fertile,
well-drained garden soil, in dappled shade.
❦ PLANT CARE Protect the bulbs of the lilies
from mice. Stake foxgloves in late spring, and
remove spent flower spires to encourage side-
shoot flowering. Feverfew and lady's mantle
must be controlled since both self-seed freely;
remove unwanted plants regularly.

FEVERFEW
Tanacetum parthenium
This has been used as a general
tonic and arthritis treatment for
centuries. Leaves are known to aid
some migraine sufferers, although
● they may cause mouth ulcers.

LADY'S MANTLE
Alchemilla mollis
As its common name
suggests, this herb
has long treated
female complaints.
Young leaves are
● delicious in salads.

A Collection of Old Favorites

THESE ARE OLD FAVORITES for good reasons – judgment lies in performance, and these are the plants that have won out with the quality of their flowers, their shape and form, and their staying power, often over many centuries. You may be surprised to discover that they are herbs, yet all have their uses.

CAT'S FAVORITE

The top of a low wall is ideal for the sprawling catmint, Nepeta x faassenii. *At this height you can appreciate its lovely flowers and inhale its aroma. It is good for soothing the digestion as well as exciting cats.*

WOODLAND GROWERS

Foxgloves are incredibly beautiful biennials, whose poisonous leaves give us drugs to combat heart disease. They grow best in semishade, adequately provided here by a birch, which has lovely dappled bark.

HEADY SUMMER SCENT

Honeysuckle, especially Lonicera periclymenum 'Serotina', *has a long flowering season. Its sweet, pervasive scent of nutmeg carries well in the air. It is used in cough mixtures for its expectorant qualities.*

HOLLYHOCK
Alcea rosea 'Nigra'
This biennial is related to
marsh mallow, *Althaea
officinalis*, and has similar
properties – an extract
soothes coughs and sore
throats. The flowers of
Alcea rosea, which yield
dyes, may be red, pink,
white, or yellow. •

Gardener's Notes

These tall favorites are shown off to their best
advantage against a wall. Both indigo and myrtle
flower over a long period all summer long.
Hollyhocks can be grown as annuals or biennials.
❦ SITE & SOIL Plant in rich, moist, well-drained
soil in a sunny, sheltered position away from cool
winds. The myrtle, like the hollyhocks, can grow
to 10ft (3m) and the indigo to 6ft (2m).
❦ PLANT CARE In dry summers, make sure that the
myrtle is kept adequately watered. Hollyhocks are
easy to grow from seed but may not come true.
For a second flowering the following year, cut
down hollyhock flowers as soon as they are over.

• MYRTLE
Myrtus luma
Much-loved by the Romans,
this ancient plant produces
its sweetly fragrant flowers
from late spring on. Leaves
and fruits, also used as an
antiseptic and astringent, are
delicious cooked with game.

INDIGO
Indigofera heterantha
From midsummer until
midautumn this beautiful
deciduous shrub with fernlike leaves is strewn with
pink flowers. Leaves and
stems, particularly those of
I. tinctoria and *I. arrecta*,
• yield blue dye.

Flames of Summer

IT IS A COMMON MISCONCEPTION that herbs are rather dull-looking plants, utilitarian and not very attractive. Not at all! Most herbs hold their own with other decorative plants in the garden. Here, as proof, is a show of pale and brilliant pink, and yellow and orange-red. Both make a vibrant display for the back or middle of a border.

IN THE PINK

In high summer, a pale sea of yarrow, Achillea millefolium *'Cerise Queen', contrasts dramatically with the brilliant spires of loosestrife,* Lythrum salicaria *'The Beacon'. They make easy, stylish companions.*

Gardener's Notes

An exciting and vibrant harmony of orange-red and yellow is captured in this very special border mix of butterfly weed and tansy.

❧ SITE & SOIL These hardy perennials both thrive in poor, very well-drained soil in a sunny position. Soil that is too rich will inhibit flowering.

❧ PLANT CARE Cut back tansy to control it or choose a compact alternative such as *Tanacetum vulgare* var. *crispum* which has finer, feathery leaves.

TANSY •
Tanacetum vulgare
All plant parts are sharply aromatic. Its bitter leaves were used during Lent for tansy cakes and custards. The toxic oil, not to be taken internally, is used homeopathically to treat scabies and threadworms.

• BUTTERFLY WEED
Asclepias tuberosa
A root extract is used to clear pleurisy and bronchitis, a function implied by the plant's alternative name, pleurisy root.

Summer Border

THE GARDEN IS UNSTOPPABLE NOW. Each plant seems to be crying out for attention as it parades its glory. In the borders, a rainbow of color explodes, and culinary herbs are at their best, before leaves become tough and less tasty. Choose your herbs for their shapes and hues; set off spires against mounds, light against dark.

ON THE WILD SIDE

A tempestuous planting of white mugwort, Artemisia lactiflora, *spires of mullein,* Verbascum bombyciferum, *and the gangly Scots thistle,* Onopordum acanthium, *is fronted by variegated spearmint in flower.*

SILVER-PINK PLANTING

The soft pink of Sidalcea 'Sussex Beauty' *is intensified by its juxtaposition with silver-gray poppy heads and mugwort,* Artemisia ludoviciana, *and dark pink loosestrife,* Lythrum salicaria.

ORBS AND SPIRES

The brilliant spires of loosestrife, Lythrum salicaria 'Firecandle', *contrast with the imposing globes of* Echinops ritro. *Ripened heads of poppy,* Papaver somniferum, *can just be seen in the background.*

Gardener's Notes

At its most impressive in the height of summer, this
beautifully varied mix of shapes and forms ranges
from statuesque Joe-pye weed, through poisonous but
pretty monkshood to lower-growing khella.
Joe-pye weed is a vigorous grower and must be
planted at the back of the border. Monkshood
flower spires can be almost as tall.

❦ SITE & SOIL Plant in well-drained but
moist soil in sun or partial shade.

❦ PLANT CARE Best treated as an annual,
the seeds of hardy khella should
be planted in spring. Always
wash your hands well after
handling monkshood.

MONKSHOOD ●
Aconitum napellus
This highly poisonous
but very decorative plant
is used by qualified
herbalists as a sedative
and pain killer. The
flowers, leaves, stalks,
and roots are all toxic.

JOE-PYE WEED ●
Eupatorium purpureum
The flowers are sweet-
scented and leaves are
apple-scented, but it is
the rhizomes that treat
cystitis, urethritis, and
kidney problems.

KHELLA ●
Ammi visnaga
All parts of this extremely
decorative plant, with its
whorls of white flowers and
feathery foliage, are aromatic.
It is used to treat asthma and
other respiratory problems.

Rustic Golden Meadow

MANY GOLDEN-FLOWERED HERBS have a rustic appearance. With this in mind, plant a group of them to produce a meadowlike collage in a wide border or a larger wild area. They enjoy sunshine and repay with a sunny show that persists throughout summer and into autumn.

YELLOW AND GREEN THEME
The tall spires of yellow hollyhocks, Alcea rosea, *whose flowers in infusion treat sore throats, here vie for attention with* Bupleurum fruticosum, Chrysanthemum coronarium, Nicotiana *'Lime Green', and the mullein,* Verbascum bombyciferum.

GOLDEN MOUNDS
Against a soft green background of hops, Humulus lupulus, *a foam of lady's mantle,* Alchemilla mollis, *mixes with feathery southernwood,* Artemisia abrotanum, *motherwort,* Leonurus cardiaca, *rue,* Ruta graveolens, *and white mallow,* Malva moschata *'Alba'.*

EVENING PRIMROSE •
Oenothera biennis
The flowers of this sweet-scented biennial open in the evening. Among its many herbal uses, it is a general tonic, aids sleep, and is a skin treatment.

LOVAGE •
Levisticum officinale
The young leaves have a sharp, celery-like flavor and are delicious in salads and soups. Infusions ease indigestion or serve as a gargle for sore throats.

YARROW •
Achillea 'Coronation Gold'
Much more decorative in appearance than common yarrow, 'Coronation Gold' has similar properties. A leaf infusion aids digestion, and an extract helps wounds and sores to heal.

YELLOW DOCK
Rumex crispus
Dock roots clear
toxins to soothe
skin irritations
and stimulate
the liver. •

Gardener's Notes

This planting has a haphazard appearance; it would
make a particularly interesting addition to a border in
the wild garden. All are medium- to tall-growing herbs,
and best planted toward the back of a border where
they will give a long-lasting sunny show.
❦ SITE & SOIL Plant in the sun in well-drained garden
soil where all the plants can freely self-seed.
❦ PLANT CARE The only concern with this unfussy mix
is keeping such vociferous self-seeders in check.

• FENNEL
Foeniculum vulgare
This versatile herb
has both medicinal
and culinary uses.
The leaves taste
very good with fish
and chicken.

Stately Sun-lovers

Many herbs have their origins in the Mediterranean, so it is not very surprising that a significant number of them enjoy sunny positions. We are familiar with rosemary, lavender, sage, thyme, and marjoram, but taller sun-loving herbs of stately proportions also proliferate, animating our gardens with their striking forms.

HEIGHT AT THE BACK

Tall and sturdy with yellow daisy-flowers and large bold green leaves, elecampane, Inula helenium, *is ideal against a wall at the back of a border. The roots are used to treat bronchitis, pleurisy, and congestion.*

LOFTY ANGELICA

The great flower heads of Angelica archangelica *stand proud above the foliage of fennel,* Foeniculum vulgare, *golden marjoram,* Origanum onites *'Aureum', and apple mint,* Mentha suaveolens.

GRACEFUL SPIRES

A spiky customer, bear's breeches, Acanthus spinosus, *has beautiful spires of hooded flowers. These rise above elegant foliage, effective in treating burns, and are here teamed with masterwort,* Astrantia major.

Gardener's Notes

Like a reflection of the sun itself, the great sunflower vies for rays of warmth with purple-headed, silver-leaved globe artichokes. Together they make an eye-catching display, with the sunflowers reaching a height of 10ft (3m) or more and the globe artichokes, 6ft (2m).

❦ SITE & SOIL Grow these bold companions in fertile, well-drained soil in a sunny, open position to give height at the back of a border.

❦ PLANT CARE Grow sunflowers from seed – they will reach a good height in one summer season and require staking. Divide globe artichokes, or sow seed in spring.

SUNFLOWER •
Helianthus annuus
The seeds are commercially harvested to make a culinary oil. This oil can also be used as a massage for arthritis and rheumatism. Add lightly roasted seeds to bread or sprinkle on salads.

GLOBE ARTICHOKE •
Cynara scolymus
Young flower heads have been considered a culinary delicacy for centuries. Leaves and flower heads treat liver complaints and lower cholesterol levels.

Opulent Fruits

FROM LATE SUMMER INTO WINTER, herbal berries and fruits are at their most beautiful. Many that we think of as plants of the field can be garden herbs of great quality and plentiful provision. Use in borders, as specimens, or even in simple hedges, and choose forms for their leaf colors, scented flowers, and sumptuous fruits.

APPLE HARVEST

The small striking fruits of this crabapple, Malus 'Cowichan', stand out dramatically against the bare branches. Tart in flavor, they make excellent jelly to be served with pork, strong meats, and game.

THORN ON FIRE

Pyracanthas are viciously spiny, but they compensate for this by producing pretty flowers followed by scarlet, orange, or golden berries in great profusion. A leaf and berry extract helps to draw out boils.

AUTUMN CONTRAST

The maroon berries of St. John's wort, Hypericum androsaemum, darken to black and make a fine autumn picture set against the dark foliage of boxwood. These berries and the aromatic leaves are diuretic.

SEASONAL BEAUTY

Guelder rose, Viburnum opulus, makes a large shrub and bears lace-cap hydrangea-like flowers in early summer. Its lobed leaves turn a beautiful red in autumn when the vivid, succulent red berries appear.

Gardener's Notes

When planning our borders we must consider how the plants will flower and fruit through the year, and how their shapes combine to form mounds and valleys, groundcovers, and overhangs. This group provides medium- and higher-level interest throughout summer and autumn. As a bonus, both the rose and crabapple have well-scented flowers.

❧ SITE & SOIL Plant in well-drained garden soil in sun or bright partial shade. Grow where the autumn evening sun will catch the red leaves of the viburnum and the red stalks and golden foliage of the pokeweed.

❧ PLANT CARE Little maintenance is needed apart from shaping the plants by trimming and removing straggly growth.

CRABAPPLE
Malus species
The autumn fruits of these small- to medium-sized deciduous trees are sharp, sometimes bitter. A purée of the fruit treats diarrhea. •

POKEWEED
Phytolacca americana
This plant is poisonous, so it is best used by qualified herbalists only. An expectorant, it has also been found to boost the immune system. •

GUELDER ROSE
Viburnum opulus
The scarlet berries of this large deciduous shrub are toxic until cooked. The bark is used to relieve cramps and muscle spasms. •

RUGOSA ROSE
Rosa rugosa
These large roses have sweet-scented flowers, healthy foliage, and large tomato-like hips, rich in vitamin C. Syrup made from these hips improves circulation. •

In the Deep Midwinter

EVEN IN THE COLDEST WEATHER, a few stalwart evergreens lend color to our gardens. Although they take up a lot of water from the soil nearby, lower-growing conifers are attractive in borders. Tall conifers such as Scots pine and silver fir are suitable for growing only in large borders; they also make excellent specimens for large gardens.

LEOPARD'S BANE

Doronicum pardalianches *was reported by herbalist Gerard as "killing Panthers, Swine, Wolves, and all kinds of wilde beasts." All parts are toxic, but its attractive leaves and summer flowers enhance any border.*

SILVER CHILL

Silver fir, Abies alba, is suitable for growing in a large bed where there is plenty of space. Oil distilled from the resin acts as an expectorant for coughs and asthma. Resin is used in turpentine.

Gardener's Notes

Most conifers tolerate the cold of winter well. With this group, bear in mind that the cedar and Scots pine eventually make forest-sized trees, so they will need to be planted at the back of a really large border. The others have thick foliage at their bases, creating good screens.

❧ SITE & SOIL Plant in well-drained acid or neutral soil since pines and spruces dislike alkaline conditions. They all prefer sun and will withstand exposed positions.

❧ PLANT CARE Conifers are sometimes neglected; fortunately many excel with little attention. Tough as they are, make sure they do not dry out excessively in their first summers, and feed the young plants each year in spring.

BLUE CEDAR ●
Cedrus atlantica f. *glauca*
The ancient Egyptians used the oil as embalming fluid. Now, the oil is a bronchial inhalant and an ingredient in perfumery. Place its fragrant wood in drawers and cupboards to deter moths.

SCOTS PINE •
Pinus sylvestris
Oil made from the aromatic
cones-and needles of this 65ft
(20m) red-barked tree is used
in perfumes and as an inhalant
for respiratory problems.

SAVIN JUNIPER
Juniperus sabina var. *tamariscifolia*
A decorative wide-spreading plant
that is extremely poisonous. Its oil
is used for veterinary purposes. •

ARIZONA CYPRESS
Cupressus glabra
This has aromatic silvery
leaves, and red-brown
stems. Its oil is used in
making perfumes and for
bath oils. Inhaled, it
treats coughs. •

Winter Outlines

By LEAVING MANY HERBS intact at the end of their season, you can create winter outlines of incredible beauty. In borders or island beds of specimen plants, the bare bones of trees, stems, seed heads, and berries sketch patterns against the ground or sky, particularly atmospheric when there is snow or frost on the ground.

FROSTED FENNEL

In winter, the dry stems and seeds of fennel, Foeniculum vulgare, *take on delicate hoary shapes that cheer the eye. A sixteenth century herbalist suggested further benefits to the visual sense: "Of Fennell, Roses, Vervain, Rue, and Celandine, is made a water good to cleere the sight of eine."*

CRABAPPLE •
Malus 'Red Sentinel'
The fruits of the crab-apple ripen in autumn and last into winter. If the birds do not get them first, they make a jelly preserve, delicious with dark and rich meats.

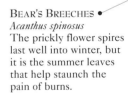

BEAR'S BREECHES •
Acanthus spinosus
The prickly flower spires last well into winter, but it is the summer leaves that help staunch the pain of burns.

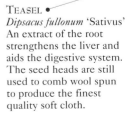

TEASEL •
Dipsacus fullonum 'Sativus'
An extract of the root strengthens the liver and aids the digestive system. The seed heads are still used to comb wool spun to produce the finest quality soft cloth.

SUMAC IN SNOW

The dramatic winter form of sumac, Rhus typhina, wonderful here as a specimen tree, can also be a major player in a large border.

BIRDS' WINTER FARE

This prickly rugosa rose makes an excellent meal for birds when the ground is frozen and snow covered, and food is difficult to find.

● MISTLETOE
Viscum album
This ancient evergreen plant is a
parasite on trees, particularly oak,
apple, and hawthorn. It aids the
immune system, has sedative
properties, and makes an ointment
for treating rheumatism and arthritis.

● SILVER BIRCH
Betula pendula
A leaf and bark extract is of benefit
to both rheumatism and arthritis
sufferers. The oil treats eczema.

● OLD MAN'S BEARD
Clematis vitalba
This rampant climber with
its decorative seed heads is
poisonous. A very small
quantity of leaf extract is
used externally to treat pain
from sores and blisters.

Gardener's Notes

An intriguing mix of twigs, spikes,
seeds, fruits, and bark is well suited
to an informal large border. There, the
teasels will not be a nuisance, bear's
breeches will form clumps, and old
man's beard can scramble unhindered
through the crabapple or a tall hedge.
❧ SITE & SOIL This selection of plants
is not fussy about soil, but they do
prefer a bright spot with a reasonable
amount of sunshine.
❧ PLANT CARE To propagate mistletoe,
lodge the sticky seed in a small cut made
into the underside of the bark; most
deciduous trees – especially apples – are
suitable. It may take up to ten years for
the mistletoe to flower. Be careful: the
spikes on dried bear's breeches flower
spires are sharp. Pick the crabapples to
make jelly before the birds get them all.

FEATURES

WHILE PLANTS ARE THE UNDISPUTED stars in a garden, features are the
ideal devices to spell out a resting spot, cause an exclamation, or
simply give someplace to take a short pause. Every herb garden
should have a place for sitting and delighting in your herbal paradise,
or at the very least a focal point to complement your chosen plants.

Seats, along with statues, arches, urns, and arbors, can greatly enhance your garden and set off the plants that fill it.

The all-important place to sit offers plenty of scope for impressive features, from a larger dedicated seating area where you can entertain friends and family, to a lone chair that can be moved around as seasonal highlights, or the time of day, dictate. Many seats and benches are decorative in their own right and make fine focal points in the herb garden.

I always try to introduce some water into the garden – even if it is only a small trough or basin. Gently moving water is even better, with its soothing murmurings. Still water in a pool also beckons and entices, demanding your attention. Liquid reflections can be mesmeric; constantly changing as the breeze ruffles the water and the images break up and reorganize themselves.

Be sure not to overlook the beauty of the garden at night: an arbor or arch covered in fragrant, flowering climbers, surrounded by aromatic shrubs and perennials, makes for a feature that is rewarding to visit any time of day, but especially after dusk when many of the scented herbs smell strongly.

A come-hither view to a statue rising from a mound of aromatics, an urn spilling over with flowering herbs, or a simple sundial, all draw you closer to smell, to see the colors, to touch and coax the scent from the leaves, thus making sure that you fully appreciate and savor the herbs in your garden.

△ POOL OF DELIGHT
*A brick-edged pool plays host to waterlilies,
sweet flag, and lady's mantle. Fragrant
waterlilies of varying sizes are available.*

◁ GOTHIC PLEASURES
*Not everyone has such a resplendent place to
sit, but we can still enjoy the scent of climbing
honeysuckle from the simplest of seats.*

TIMELY RETREAT ▷
*An herb garden is just the place for a sundial.
Surround it with a tapestry of Mediterranean
herbs, at their happiest in the heat of the day.*

Tranquil Retreat

YOUR GARDEN should be a place to relax in, so make time to enjoy its magic, and allow the plants to awaken your senses. Surround seating areas with herbs in cool, serene-colored hues, add the sound of running water and soft wind chimes, and you will have created a retreat where you can feel calm and uplifted.

PLANT FOR PASSION
Vigorous and moderately hardy, passion vine is a most appropriate garland for our special seat. Passiflora caerulea *is wondrous, with intricately detailed, sweet-scented flowers from midsummer to autumn.*

CORNFLOWERS •
Centaurea cyanus
The intense blue color is extracted from the flowers of this annual for use in paint and ink pigments. An infusion of the flowers makes an eye wash for sore or tired eyes.

A PLACE TO DAYDREAM
Add a few cushions to this rustic seat and drift away. The gentle herbs around it include wall germander, Teucrium chamaedrys, *boxwood,* Buxus sempervirens, *and bear's breeches,* Acanthus spinosus.

STOCKS
Matthiola incana
These are a must for the
decorative herb garden, with
one of the strongest scents of
all plants. The flowers are used
in commercial perfumery, and
• can be added to potpourri.

Gardener's Notes

A group of annual beauties chosen for their cool
colors and, of course, their scent. Love-in-a-mist has
clear, pale blue flowers, with a decorative ruff of fine
green bracts, followed by seed heads. Cornflowers, a
field flower that readily self-seeds, are an intense rich
blue. Soft cream stocks, with their spicy-fragranced
flowers, complement the blues perfectly.

❦ SITE & SOIL This simple set needs sun and a rich,
well-drained soil, kept
just moist in summer.

❦ PLANT CARE These
plants will all flower
from seed in one
season, although the
stocks can be treated
as biennials. If growing
stocks from seed,
choose a variety that
is resistant to mildew.

• LOVE-IN-A-MIST
Nigella damascena
This herb is used
commercially in
perfumery. A seed
infusion benefits
the digestion.

Restful Perfumes

To sit engulfed in the sweet and aromatic scents of herbs is a treat
to be savored in a herb garden. If your bench is against a house or
garden wall, surround it with fragrant climbers such as rose, jasmine,
or honeysuckle. Even if you only have a small patio, grow scented
herbs in pots around a chair or bench to give the same pleasure.

● **BELLFLOWER**
Campanula lactiflora
'Prichard's Variety'
In the 16th century, the
roots of the old-fashioned
cottage garden campanulas
were cooked and served
with oil and vinegar.

LAMB'S EARS
Stachys byzantina
Most attractive in the
herb garden, this is a
decorative cousin of
wood betony, *Stachys
officinalis*, which was
previously thought of
● as a cure for all ills.

ROSE
Rosa 'Jacques Cartier'
Repeat-flowering with
flat, quartered blooms,
this rose has an exquisite
● fruity perfume.

Gardener's Notes

Roses, those most voluptuous of flowers, are some of the most perfumed plants of all, especially the old-fashioned varieties. They mix well with perennials and lower shrubs, in fact any plants that help disguise the unshapely growth of most roses. I like mixing them with lavenders, lower-growing rosemary, catmint, lavender cotton, artemisias, campanulas, and lamb's ears.

❧ SITE & SOIL Grow in rich, moist, well-drained soil. All prefer sun, but will put on a good show in semishade too.

❧ PLANT CARE Feed perpetual-flowering roses after their first flush has finished to encourage more flowers. Cut back catmint for a second flowering.

ROSE
Rosa 'Ferdinand Pichard'
As with all fragrant roses, the petals of this highly scented, repeat-flowering rose can be used with lemon to make a refreshing infusion, served
• in salads, or crystallized.

ROSE
Rosa 'The Dark Lady'
A modern English rose that is perpetual and intensely perfumed. Try making a preserve from its petals with
• jasmine flowers and lemon.

SWEET SPICES

Drifting overhead, the nutmeg-scented flowers of woodbine, Lonicera periclymenum *'Serotina', spice the air around this seat, making it the perfect spot for dreamy contemplation from midsummer until autumn.*

• CATMINT
Nepeta mussinii
An infusion of the aromatic leaves is a sleep-inducing night drink and is taken for mild stomachaches. The plant causes euphoria in cats.

HEADY AROMAS

What better than a seat set among a sea of rosemary and lavender? Here Rosmarinus officinalis *and* Lavandula angustifolia *'Hidcote' grow, but many cultivars of both species are available to choose from.*

Arbors & Arches

To walk through an arch or sit in an arbor, surrounded by beauty and attended by wonderful scents is indeed a delight. Herbal climbers – confederate jasmine, roses, hops, passion vine – create a terrestrial heaven, and at ground level myriad perfumed shrubs, perennials, and annuals make their contribution.

SUMMER IDYLL

Such temptation, for what could be more enticing than this arbor with a canopy of climbing roses, set about with yellow hollyhocks, pink mallow and loosestrife, and silver artemisia.

LEMON BALM
Melissa officinalis 'Aurea'
The strongly lemon-scented leaves of this perennial are used to make a comforting tisane that is of benefit to the digestion. The plant also makes an effective insect repellent.

GOLDEN ARCHWAY

The shapely leaves of this hop plant, Humulus lupulus, *will clothe an archway or arbor in one season. In pillows, dried bracts from female plants aid sleep. Hops are also a main ingredient in beer production.*

Gardener's Notes

This intensely perfumed group is well suited to adorning an arbor. Both lemon verbena, which should be planted where it can be brushed against, and confederate jasmine, which reaches 12ft (4m), are a little tender.

❦ SITE & SOIL Grow in good, well-drained garden soil, preferably not alkaline, in a sunny position. The scents will be particularly intoxicating at night, so place a seat close by where you can enjoy them to the full.

❦ PLANT CARE Remove all dead flower heads to encourage more flowers. In cooler areas, plant lemon verbena and confederate jasmine in pots, to move to a frost-free site in winter.

CONFEDERATE JASMINE
Trachelospermum jasminoides
A slightly tender evergreen climber, with abundant highly scented flowers throughout summer, used in Chinese medicine to treat arthritis.

LEMON VERBENA
Aloysia triphylla
The strongest of all lemon-scented plants, its dried leaves are used in potpourri and sachets. A leaf infusion makes a soothing tea.

YARROW
Achillea millefolium
This ancient herb was used by Achilles' army to heal battle wounds, hence its name. It is an expectorant, reduces fever, and is taken to ease indigestion.

GOLDEN OREGANO
Origanum vulgare 'Aureum'
Another fragrant favorite, whose sweetly aromatic leaves enhance most savory Mediterranean dishes. An infusion treats colds and congestion and eases most types of stomach upset.

Sweet Repose

SEATS IN THE GARDEN, when carefully positioned, can provide
an essential vantage point from which to enjoy the fruits of your
labors. Consider whether you want one that can be easily moved
about to catch and admire seasonal shows as they come and go, or
a more permanent one that stays where it has a year-round view.

EVENING PERFORMANCE
Grow the beautiful evening primrose, Oenothera biennis, *beside a
summer seat so that you can watch the scented flowers open as the sun
goes down. Seed oil improves the skin and notably benefits eczema.*

Gardener's Notes

Several color forms of yarrow have been bred
in reds, pinks, apricots, and yellows. Here it
is mixed with turtlehead to make a colorful
seat-side show, flowering over a long period
starting with the lemon-scented yarrow in early
summer, and continuing and overlapping with
pink- or white-flowered turtlehead, which
blooms from midsummer into autumn. Both
plants grow to about 30in (75cm), so are ideal
plants to surround a sunny bench.
❧ SITE & SOIL Grow in a sunny position (the
turtlehead tolerates some shade) in good, well-
drained soil. Both perennials, they would also
be ideal for the middle or front of a border.
❧ PLANT CARE Deadhead yarrow to encourage
further flowering, and divide larger clumps in
spring. Divide turtlehead in autumn or spring.

MIDSUMMER VIEW
*A moveable chair placed at the edge of a lawn (under a bower of
scented 'Albertine' climbing roses for heightened pleasure) can afford
good views of the garden. What better place to enjoy the summer sun?*

TURTLEHEAD •
Chelone obliqua
An infusion of this lovely
perennial benefits the
digestive system and
tones the liver.

• YARROW
Achillea millefolium
'Cerise Queen' and
A. 'Moonlight' Both are
attractive forms of unshowy
field yarrow. An infusion is
good for colds and fevers,
and it aids digestion.

Glowing Autumn Herbs

EACH SEASON HAS ITS OWN color palette, and in autumn the glowing reds, rusts, ambers, and golds come to the fore. These warm shades highlight the honeyed colors of features in terra-cotta and stone. With the onset of cold, leaves become brilliant emblems of the summer's end, as do a starry cast of herbal autumn flowers.

BETWEEN THE SEASONS

With the promise of fragrant winter flowers soon to follow, soothing witch hazel, Hamamelis virginiana, *puts on a brave autumn show of golden yellow leaves. Below, in a seasonal contrast, the terra-cotta herb jar of thymes still looks green and summery.*

Gardener's Notes

Borders can be full of life and color in autumn. Here, deep blood-red roses, crushed orange chrysanthemums, crackling yellow goldenrod, and rich green and silver elaeagnus make a vibrant display around this stone urn.

❦ SITE & SOIL Grow in a sunny position in well-drained, rich soil.

❦ PLANT CARE Fertilize roses in spring, and again after each flush of flowers. Feed and water chrysanthemums well until the flower buds are formed in late summer. A hybrid goldenrod such as 'Goldenmosa' or 'Lemore' will be less invasive than the species.

ROSE •
Rosa 'Mme. Louis Laperrière'
A perpetual-flowering rose that is highly scented. Crystallize the petals for decorating desserts, make a rose water infusion, or mix with jasmine flowers and lemons to make a preserve.

CHRYSANTHEMUM •
Chrysanthemum 'Gloria'
The petals of this medium-height perennial can be added to salads. Medicinally, the flowers relieve arterial problems and angina.

SWEET TANGERINE

The long flowering season of French marigold, Tagetes patula, *continues from summer to the first autumn frosts. A friend to many plants, its sulfurous roots keep eelworms (nematodes) and certain weeds at bay. It, too, would look good around the urn opposite.*

GOLDENROD
Solidago virgaurea
A poultice of this fast-
growing perennial is
applied externally to sores
and wounds. Internally, a
decoction soothes coughs,
sore throats, and fevers, and
treats kidney problems. ●

ELAEAGNUS
Elaeagnus pungens
Edible autumn fruits follow the intensely
perfumed autumn flowers of this
evergreen shrub. It
can be used to
treat asthma. ●

Burning Embers

AUTUMN IS A SEASON that seems to burn itself out. We are led from the brilliant incandescent haze of late summer through a display of orange and red flames, then softly glowing embers, finally to the bare brown remains that characterize the winter months. The fiery autumn herbs shown here all harmonize well with warm terra-cotta.

RED AGAINST GREEN

A warm color against a large expanse of a cool color makes the warm color leap out. Thus it is with the startling combination of scarlet Crataegus laevigata *haws against tree ivy,* Hedera helix.

BRIGHT LANTERNS

This startling muddle of glowing colors really shines. Orange lanterns of Physalis alkekengi *and orange-red hips of* Rosa californica *'Plena' contrast brightly with the plum red of* Sedum spectabile *'Meteor'.*

FRUITS AND FOLIAGE

This combination of Rosa wilmottiae *and* Cotinus coggygria *'Foliis Purpureis' is a winner all year round. Together they offer fragrance, attractive stems and flowers, and, here in autumn, foliage and fruits.*

ORIENTAL BITTERSWEET •
Celastrus orbiculatus
An extract from this hardy deciduous
climber benefits the circulation
and aids digestion. Tiny
summer flowers give
way to the fruit.

CLERODENDRUM •
Clerodendrum trichotomum
This small deciduous tree
bears many fragrant jasmine-
like flowers in late summer;
the decorative berries follow.
In decoction, the plant treats
rheumatism and arthritis.

Gardener's Notes

A terra-cotta statue is surrounded by
unusual autumn herbs. She stands
amidst a fiery mix of chrysanthemums
and prince's feather. Cascading behind
her are the green leaves and curious berries of
clerodendrum, while the striking orange and
yellow fruits of bittersweet, which grows
to 30ft (10m) tall, hover around her head.
❧ SITE & SOIL Plant in a rich well-drained
soil in a sunny position. Clerodendrum
prefers a sheltered site, out of wind.
❧ PLANT CARE Plant out the
annual prince's feather in early
summer. For bittersweet to fruit,
grow both male and female
plants. Clerodendrum is often
many-stemmed, so select
a strong leader to grow
it as a tree.

PRINCE'S FEATHER •
Amaranthus hypochondriacus
Seeds follow flowers in late
autumn, and are consumed as
a cereal in South America. A
plant extract controls bleeding
and treats mouth ulcers.

CHRYSANTHEMUM •
Chrysanthemum 'Brightness'
The flowers of this perennial
are used to treat arterial
problems and angina. Add
the petals to salads.

PATHS & HEDGES

A GARDEN SEEN IN ITS TOTALITY at a glance can be dull, so it is good
to create a little mystery, even in small gardens. Paths and hedges
are ideal: they excite the imagination by leading and concealing.
Both are practical too – hedges give protection and order, while
paths make culinary herbs accessible for harvest and maintenance.

Paths are always a great source of
excitement even when they are old
friends, for they lead you in a chosen
direction and, while you walk, you can
look and smell and touch the plants
around you. Herbs are among the best
pathside plants, because they often
provide sensual as well as visual treats.

The paths I like are those that mix
straight sections, allowing vistas, with
winding sections, which curve around
and through layers of plants, providing
surprises at every turn. In your own
garden, the path can provide a vantage
point to observe and enjoy your plants'
progress. In someone else's garden, a
path is a source of fascination, perhaps
leading to a secret spot.

Hedges also divide and create a
sense of mystery, but they encompass
as well, making pockets, sections, and
layers of plants. Choose deciduous
hedge plants for annual variation or
evergreens for year-round consistency.
Hedge size too can vary as you wish – a
hedge may be made from low-growing
lavender or boxwood, immensely tall
oaks, or plants that grow to somewhere
in between in height.

Hawthorn, hazel, sweetbriar roses,
and euonymus make informal country-
style hedges that provide a gentle
transition from the cultivated to the
wild; privet, yew, thuja, holly, or beech
hedges can be clipped into more
formal shapes. Hedges can establish
surprisingly rapidly: a lavender hedge is
impressive in two years, and even one
of yew or holly can be effective in five.

△ BOXED IN
*Boxwood, with its tiny dense leaves, clips
well, making it the ideal low hedge. A covering
of midwinter snow enhances its formal shape.*

◁ RICH GREEN CONIFERS
*The rich dark green of a grapefruit-scented
thuja hedge forms an excellent background
for showing off both pale and bright flowers.*

AROMATIC HERB-EDGED PATH ▷
*A wonderful path made from slabs, gravel,
and stable bricks leads between herb-strewn
beds to a seat. I wonder where it leads next?*

Graceful Pathside Companions

WE OFTEN THINK THAT ONLY low-growing plants are suited for the edges of a path or the front of a border, but this need not always be the case. I like to create mountains and valleys with my plantings, and sometimes it is good to have the mountains at the front. Take care only that taller plants do not encroach upon the path too much.

CALLA LILY
Zantedeschia elliottiana
This elegant, early summer-flowering perennial enjoys a sheltered lightly shaded site.

COMFREY
Symphytum officinale
Highly valued for its ability to heal wounds, cuts, and broken bones. Recent research reveals carcinogenic properties, so it may be best to avoid internal use.

COLUMBINE
Aquilegia vulgaris
Used homeopathically, the plant treats problems of the nervous system. A root extract is applied externally to treat skin complaints.

Gardener's Notes

This pathside group of elegant herbs all enjoy a position that is out of strong sunshine, where they will make a gentle early summer statement with their soft pastels and attractive leaves. These plants have been popular for centuries, and you can now take advantage of new decorative forms to give even more colorful interest to the garden.

❧ SITE & SOIL This group thrives in moist but well-drained, rich soil in a semishaded site.

❧ PLANT CARE Remove (and dry) long-lasting masterwort flowers, and you may be rewarded with a second flush. Divide clumps of masterwort in autumn. Columbines will self-seed, but new plants may not come true.

STRONG VERTICALS

Following their stunning flowers, poppy seed heads always catch the eye. Here they pose next to purple orach, Atriplex hortensis *var.* rubra, *whose leaves can replace sorrel for a less sharp flavor in cooking.*

• MASTERWORT
Astrantia major
This attractive perennial bears a succession of greenish white bracts from early summer. It was once thought to help reduce fevers.

SHAGGY HEADS AND ELEGANT SPIRES

For a tall, harmonizing pathside statement, grow purple loosestrife, Lythrum *'Rose Queen', in front of loftier bee balm,* Monarda *'Melissa'. Infuse bee balm leaves for a tea that benefits the digestion.*

Mellow Yellow Walk

PLANTS WITH YELLOW FLOWERS or golden foliage always look cheerful and welcoming, especially when they edge the path to a favorite seat. Scent, too, is important, so from the many herbs of this color, choose plants that release fragrance as you brush against them: golden lemon balm, mint, sage, geranium, or thyme.

Gardener's Notes

This sunny and highly perfumed group will give months of pleasure from early summer until late autumn. Not quite as lemony as lemon verbena but much hardier, the lemon balm needs only to be touched to release its fragrance. Low-growing thyme will spill onto the path; the other plants lend a bit of height behind.

❧ SITE & SOIL All these plants like well-drained garden soil in a sunny position.

❧ PLANT CARE Cut back the lemon balm in June to prevent it from setting seed and to encourage new shoots. Deadhead pot marigolds regularly.

● DILL
Anethum graveolens
This ancient herb is highly aromatic. Excellent for digestive problems, it is often used to treat colic. The leaves complement fish and chicken dishes.

POT MARIGOLD
Calendula officinalis
Medicinally, this benefits gastric and skin problems. Petals flavor and color
● rice and cakes.

LEMON BALM ●
Melissa officinalis 'Aurea'
Use the highly lemon-scented leaves to flavor sorbets and sauces. They make a comforting tisane that improves digestion, and repel insects.

● VARIEGATED THYME
Thymus x *citriodorus* 'Aureus'
The main use of this aromatic low-growing herb is culinary. Its lemon-scented leaves, also much-loved by bees, aid respiratory problems.

LEMON YELLOW MIGNONETTE

At the corner of a stone path, annual Reseda lutea *offers a multitude of sweetly fragrant flower spikes in late summer and early autumn. Its yellow flowers, good for cutting, have long been used to make dye.*

FROTH OF GOLD

Seen here spilling out its golden lime froth of flowers over a path, lady's mantle, Alchemilla mollis, *is popular with flower arrangers. Baby leaves, almost circular and extremely pretty, are eaten in salads.*

SHADY PATHSIDE

Two beautiful, rampant growers enjoy a position beside a path away from the sun. Vinca major *'Variegata', with pale lilac-blue flowers in spring, scrambles in front of ginger mint,* Mentha x gracilis *'Variegata'.*

Aromatic Shades of Green

GREEN IS RESTFUL AND EASY ON THE EYE – a color that we never get tired of. The herb world offers us a host of green leaf shades, from brilliant green, through green tinged with gold, silver, cream, white, and purple. Grow any of the aromatic, mounding selection shown here as path edging; it will provide a feast in every sense.

Gardener's Notes

Evergreen purple sage and silver rue, mixed with the spring-through-to-autumn leaves of purple mint and brilliant golden green lady's mantle, make a rich decorative and aromatic display of foliage. Lady's mantle flowers dry well.

❧ SITE & SOIL This combination looks good beside a path or the edge of a paved area. They all prefer well-drained soil in sun.

❧ PLANT CARE These herbs are all easy to grow. Lady's mantle and mint can be invasive if unchecked. Be careful when handling rue: it may cause an allergic skin reaction.

RUE
Ruta graveolens
"Herb of grace" was thought to deter serpents and protect against witchcraft and the plague.

EAU DE COLOGNE MINT
Mentha x *piperita* 'Citrata'
Not suited to savory cooking, this mint is ideal in potpourri and cosmetics, due to its eau de Cologne scent.

PURPLE SAGE •
Salvia officinalis
'Purpurascens'
Medicinally, sage is given to relieve digestive problems and to alleviate anxiety.

• LADY'S MANTLE
Alchemilla mollis
The young scalloped leaves can be infused to make a refreshing tisane.

SILVER MIX

In both texture and aroma, the contrast between these silver-leaved herbs is striking. Wormwood, Artemisia absinthium, *is feathery and lemon-scented, while sage,* Salvia officinalis, *has plain, pungent leaves.*

PURPLE AND GOLD

The tiny curled leaves of low-growing Origanum vulgare *'Aureum Crispum' are vivid gold. See how the color leaps out when grown next to the textured foliage of purple sage,* Salvia officinalis *'Purpurascens'.*

SCENTED STRIPES

Thin, curry-scented leaves of Helichrysum italicum, *minute close-knit leaves of lavender cotton,* Santolina chamaecyparissus, *and winter savory,* Satureja montana, *make an interesting year-round pattern.*

FOREVER GOLD

This golden broad-leaved thyme, Thymus pulegioides *'Aureus', is low and spreading, making it ideal for a pathside. Remember that these Mediterranean plants enjoy very well-drained soil and lots of sun.*

Low Edging

PLANTS GROWING CLOSE to a paved area, path, or lawn tend to be studied in more detail than those set farther back, so their role is crucial. Many formal and informal herbs have a front-of-bed habit and form an attractive, often aromatic edging. They also help cover soil in summer beds – I prefer it concealed – and prevent weeds.

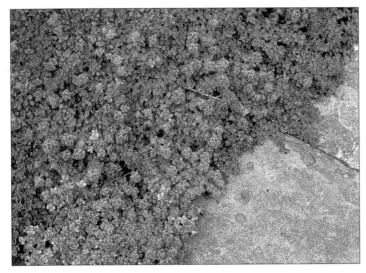

THYME FOR SPREADING
Ground-hugging Thymus serpyllum *'Minimus' grows naturally in cracks and crannies in rocky ground, so plant it in a sunny position with very well-drained soil, and it should go on a low-scale rampage.*

AROMATIC HYSSOP
Sometimes evergreen, Hyssopus officinalis *is an ideal candidate for edging. It produces lovely flower spikes for nearly three months – all summer long.*

WILD STRAWBERRY
Fragaria vesca
A beautiful and ancient plant, whose sharp-sweet fruits are delicious to eat. They are also used in the treatment of gum sores and ulcers, as well as for digestive problems. •

TUSSOCKS AND HUMMOCKS

For a sharp-scented transport of delight, pull your hand gently up a stem of lavender cotton as you pass. Like scented mignonette, Reseda lutea, next to it, its hummocks are ideal as a path or border edging.

OLD-FASHIONED INFORMALITY

The turn of this old brick path is beautifully bounded by lavender. On the right lamb's ears, Stachys byzantina, *form a silvery mat, and the boxwood pyramid is edged with germander,* Teucrium creticum.

SWEET WOODRUFF
Galium odoratum
When dried, this plant smells of hay, so in the past it was strewn as an aromatic floor covering. It reduces blood-clotting, and an infusion is good for indigestion. •

THRIFT
Armeria maritima 'Vindictive'
Thriving on cliffs and scree in the wild, this tough herb bears a long succession of flowers from early summer, above tussocks of grasslike leaves. It was once used to treat gout. •

Gardener's Notes

Wild strawberries have brilliant fluted leaves and carry delicious fruits over a long period that coincides with the thrift flowers; deep pink and red look stunning against the bright green leaves. The woodruff produces tiny white flowers in early summer, and its ruffs of leaves hold their own once the flowers have passed.

❦ SITE & SOIL Grow in good, well-drained soil in a sunny position, or one that is away from direct sun, but quite light.

❦ PLANT CARE Once established, the wild strawberry will need to be controlled since it spreads rapidly by means of runners. Remove the thrift flower heads as they die.

Sweet Scented Walkway

THE GARDEN SHOULD APPEAL to as many of the senses as possible.
When moving from one part to another, it is especially desirable
that plants on either side of the walkway smell as beautiful as they
look. Run your hand through the leaves and flowers of taller herbs
like rosemary and lemon verbena to release their essential oils.

Gardener's Notes

The perfume of this collection of low-growing pathside herbs is intoxicating in its intensity. A cocktail of clove, apricot, vanilla, camphor, and lemon scents the air, especially on sunny summer afternoons. I like to grow a good mix of hardy shrubs, perennials, and even tender annuals beside a path, to ensure both continuity and innovation each year. Night-scented stock could replace the mignonette.

❧ SITE & SOIL Grow in a sunny site in very well-drained, medium-rich, neutral to alkaline soil.

❧ PLANT CARE Deadhead pinks regularly. Sow mignonette seed where it is to flower in spring. Thin as necessary. Replace thymes with rooted cuttings every three years.

● THYME
Thymus serpyllum
This low, evergreen sub-shrub has strongly lemon-scented leaves and is an excellent culinary herb. Medicinally, it is good for coughs, sore throats, and digestive complaints.

● MIGNONETTE
Reseda odorata
The flowers of this low-growing annual are powerfully sweet-scented. Beloved of butterflies and bees, its essential oil is used in expensive perfumes.

● PINKS
Dianthus plumarius
Many of these short-lived perennials have a strong clove perfume. They were once added to liqueurs, said to calm the nerves. The lower, white part of the petal is bitter, but the top end can be added to salads.

PURPLE SAGE ●
Salvia officinalis 'Purpurascens'
When used in small quantities the pungent leaves taste especially good with pork, veal, liver, and game dishes. An infusion aids nervous and digestive problems.

CAT'S CRADLE

The apple trees along this walkway are underplanted with catmint, which sends cats into a delirium of happiness. They love to lie in it. Cut back after the first flowering, and it will produce a good second flush.

COTTAGE PATHWAY

This flagged path between mounds of sage, lavender, and lemon balm is simplicity itself, but it is a treat to walk through even in winter when the evergreen leaves can be coaxed to release their essence of summer scent.

BEST OF BASIL

Delicious with tomatoes or as Pesto Genovese with pasta, both the plain green basil, Ocimum basilicum, *and its various forms with colored and ruffled leaves – here 'Purpurascens' – have excellent flavor.*

THYME AT YOUR SIDE

Lemon thyme, Thymus x citriodorus, *is a low-growing, evergreen sub-shrub with many whorls of lilac-pink flowers in summer. The lemon-flavored leaves are particularly delicious with veal and tuna dishes.*

Informal Cottage Hedge

IF YOU HAVE SPACE, an informal hedge of rugosa roses is a must. These specimens make strong-growing and particularly disease-free shrubs with thorny stems and scented flowers. Consider too, hedges of hawthorn, dog roses, and hazel, or a mixture of them. Remember, the more they are trimmed the fewer flowers they bear.

Gardener's Notes

Plant a hedge of these rugosa roses and you will have a scented paradise, because their heady, exceedingly sweet, fruity perfumes carry well in the air. Give them plenty of space: they grow to a width and height of 6ft (2m) or more. Their foliage is lush; their flowers, produced in very large numbers over a long period, are beautifully colored; and their late summer and autumn hips are highly decorative.

❧ SITE & SOIL Plant 5ft (1.5m) apart in a staggered line in good, well-drained, sunny or semi-shaded soil. If you want to grow only one variety, I recommend 'Hansa'.

❧ PLANT CARE Feed in late spring with a good rose fertilizer for best results. Trim at the same time, but only to keep the shape.

RUGOSA ROSE
Rosa rugosa 'Alba'
This rose has single, highly scented white flowers followed by orange hips as large as tomatoes. The hips
● are rich in vitamin C.

RUGOSA ROSE
Rosa 'Blanc Double de Coubert'
The semidouble flowers are extremely perfumed, but this rose only occasionally sets fruit. A petal infusion helps digestion
● and improves circulation.

WILD HAWTHORN

Plants in this neglected hedge of hawthorn Crataegus monogyna *have reverted to their tree qualities. Because they have not been trimmed, they are in impressive full flower; the typical bright red haws will follow.*

HEDGE OF HIPS

Old man's beard, Clematis vitalba, *straggles a wild hedge interspersed with the hips of dog rose,* Rosa canina. *To support the vigorous growth of old man's beard, a hedge needs to be large.*

● RUGOSA ROSE
Rosa 'Hansa'
This very floriferous rose yields a good crop of hips and has a glorious scent that makes the petals ideal for potpourri and crystallizing. Combine the hips with crabapples to make a delicious preserve.

Silver Filigree

A HIGH PROPORTION OF AROMATIC HERBS have silver foliage, usually decorative and often resembling delicate lace. Many of these herbs make attractive edging plants, and are especially beautiful when planted among flowers in the pink, mauve-lilac, and purple range, colors that also feature prominently in the herb world.

COSMOPOLITAN MIX
Silver spikes of Dutch lavender, Lavandula 'Vera', *jostle for space with Russian tarragon,* Artemisia dracunculoides. *The latter is not as refined as French tarragon, but is excellent with game and strong meat.*

LAVENDER COTTON EDGING
Mounds of aromatic lavender cotton studded with yellow buttonlike flowers are interspersed with lower-growing lavender 'Hidcote'. Their beautiful, silvery scented leaves edge a grass path leading to a bench.

CONTRASTING FOLIAGE
Feathery rue, Ruta graveolens 'Jackman's Blue', *growing against the spotted lungwort,* Pulmonaria officinalis 'Cambridge Blue', *make an engaging pathside combination. Lungwort treats pulmonary problems.*

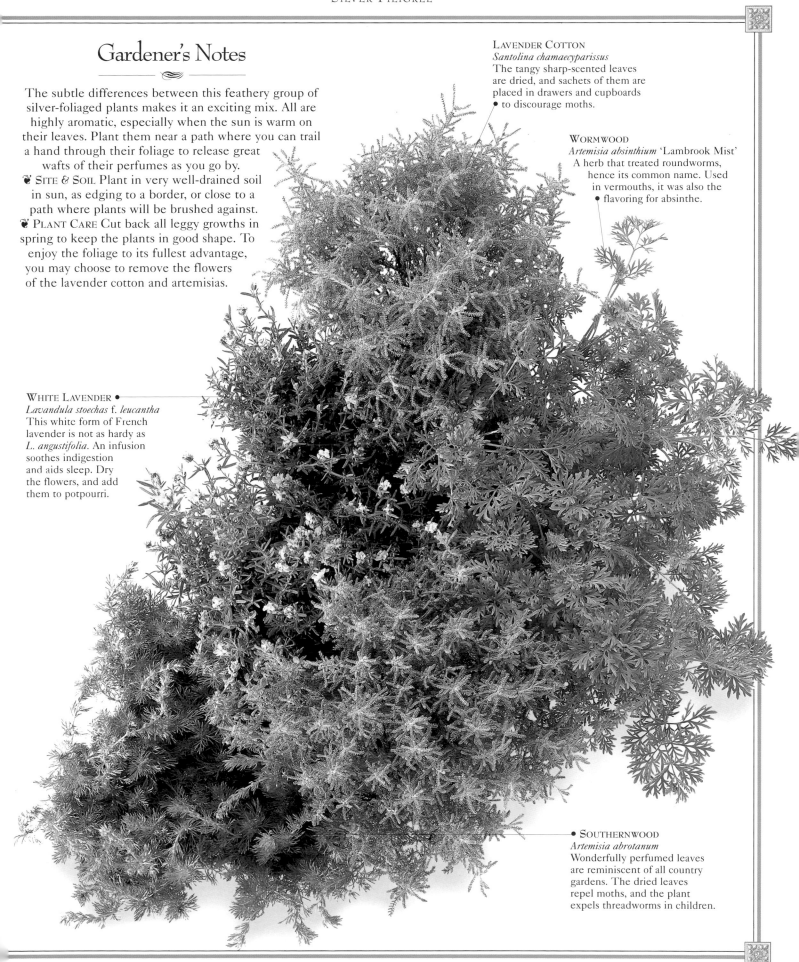

Gardener's Notes

The subtle differences between this feathery group of
silver-foliaged plants makes it an exciting mix. All are
highly aromatic, especially when the sun is warm on
their leaves. Plant them near a path where you can trail
a hand through their foliage to release great
wafts of their perfumes as you go by.
❦ SITE & SOIL Plant in very well-drained soil
  in sun, as edging to a border, or close to a
  path where plants will be brushed against.
❦ PLANT CARE Cut back all leggy growths in
spring to keep the plants in good shape. To
  enjoy the foliage to its fullest advantage,
  you may choose to remove the flowers
  of the lavender cotton and artemisias.

LAVENDER COTTON
Santolina chamaecyparissus
The tangy sharp-scented leaves
are dried, and sachets of them are
placed in drawers and cupboards
• to discourage moths.

WORMWOOD
Artemisia absinthium 'Lambrook Mist'
A herb that treated roundworms,
hence its common name. Used
in vermouths, it was also the
• flavoring for absinthe.

WHITE LAVENDER •
Lavandula stoechas f. *leucantha*
This white form of French
lavender is not as hardy as
L. angustifolia. An infusion
soothes indigestion
and aids sleep. Dry
the flowers, and add
them to potpourri.

• SOUTHERNWOOD
Artemisia abrotanum
Wonderfully perfumed leaves
are reminiscent of all country
gardens. The dried leaves
repel moths, and the plant
expels threadworms in children.

Scents of the Maquis

HOW LOVELY IT IS TO WALK between mounds and hedges of aromatic or scented herbs. These serve as re-creations of the Maquis, for immediately they transport me to the hills behind the Cote d'Azur, where stony fields are filled with lavenders, rosemarys, artemisias, sages, and santolinas, all yielding their tangy aromatic perfumes.

Gardener's Notes

Several different lavenders mixed with rosemary can make a sensational border to a path or paved area. Not only in summer, but even on a gray winter's day their silvery leaves yield that exciting scent of sunshine. All lavenders and rosemarys are aromatic, but their growing heights can vary substantially, so be sure to choose the ones that will best suit your site.

❦ SITE & SOIL Plant these Mediterranean herbs in well-drained soil in a sunny position that is not exposed to cold winter winds.

❦ PLANT CARE Dead-head lavenders for a second, smaller crop of flowers. For drying, cut just as the flowers start to come out. In spring, cut both lavenders and rosemarys back.

LAVENDER ROSEA
Lavandula angustifolia 'Rosea'
Strong-growing with highly scented flowers and leaves, this lavender is used for
● perfumes and cosmetics.

ROSEMARY
Rosmarinus officinalis
A culinary herb that is delicious with lamb and pork and, in small quantities, in apple pie. Medicinally, it benefits nervous problems such as indigestion and
● headaches.

MEDITERRANEAN PERFUMES

A wide path leading to the garden beyond is edged with hummocks of lavender cotton and lavender, in particular tall-flowering Lavandula x intermedia *'Grappenhall'. Despite its name, lavender cotton does not smell like lavender, but has a sharp, tangy fragrance.*

CLIPPED ROSEMARY HEDGE

Frequently grown as an informal shrub, versatile rosemary can also be clipped into an attractive hedge. Bear in mind that it does not live for long.

LAVENDER HIDCOTE
Lavandula angustifolia 'Hidcote'
Prescribed for problems associated with worry, such as headaches and migraines, lavenders are also used for skin and muscular problems. Use in potpourri and
• scented sachets.

• LAVENDER GRAPPENHALL
Lavandula x *intermedia* 'Grappenhall'
This, the tallest-growing lavender, is widely grown. Its long flower heads look particularly striking in a mixed lavender and rosemary hedge.

Herb Tapestry

MANY HERBS THRIVE on stony hillsides exposed to wind and sun; such culinary herbs as thyme, oregano, and sage, for example, all survive in these seemingly inhospitable sites. Replicate these conditions in paving cracks and beside paths to create colorful, aromatic foliage and flower tapestries in your own garden.

AROMATIC MARJORAMS
Two wild marjorams, Origanum vulgare *and O. vulgare var.* album, *intermingle as they spread their fragrant leafy stems and speckled flowers. In the kitchen, add leaves to meat and vegetable dishes.*

FRUITS AND FOLIAGE
The cheerful red hips of a low-growing rose are revealed amid the feathery blue waves of rue, Ruta graveolens *'Jackman's Blue'. Take care when handling rue: it may cause an allergic reaction.*

PATCHWORK PATTERNS
Silver-leaved curry plant, Helichrysum italicum, *lavender cotton,* Santolina chamaecyparissus, *purple barberry,* Berberis thunbergii *'Atropurpurea', and green boxwood weave a tapestry of subtle colors.*

FRESH FOLIAGE
Different foliage colors harmonize in this combination of variegated lemon balm and ginger mint, silvery horsemint, and golden-leaved marjoram, to give us a visual and aromatic feast as we pass by.

Gardener's Notes

Spreading herbs grown in cracks enhance any paved area, although it is best to avoid sites subjected to constant traffic; few plants other than grass, tolerate being stepped on frequently. Sage, marjoram, and thyme thrive in full sun, whereas tiny Corsican mint, and bugles flourish in shade.

❦ SITE & SOIL Choose your plant carefully to suit your site. Sun-lovers like very well-drained soil that is not too rich, while the shady specimens prefer a richer, moist but well-drained soil.

❦ PLANT CARE Shear off all thyme flowers once they are over, and since they are relatively short-lived, replace two- or three-year old plants with new ones, grown from cuttings taken in late spring.

VARIEGATED THYME •
Thymus x citriodorus
'Silver Queen'
An excellent culinary thyme, this is similar to *T. vulgaris* 'Silver Posie' but is less hardy.

• PALE PINK THYME
Thymus vulgaris
Use with bay, celery, and parsley to make bouquet garni for soups and stews. Its oil is expectorant and treats fungal infections externally.

• CORSICAN MINT
Mentha requienii
This tiny mint has a very strong peppermint scent that carries far on the air. Decorate chocolate desserts with sprigs.

• PINK THYME
Thymus serpyllum 'Pink Chintz'
The sprigs add a Mediterranean flavor to meats such as chicken, pork, and veal. An extract is used for bronchial and throat problems.

• VARIEGATED THYME
Thymus vulgaris 'Silver Posie'
The silver-edged leaves are lemon scented and are an excellent flavoring for poultry. The oil is an asthma treatment.

PURPLE BUGLE •
Ajuga reptans 'Atropurpurea'
Herbalist Ruellius wrote that "hee needs neither Physition nor Surgeon, that hath Bugle and Sanicle." Indeed, bugle is a painkiller and staunches both internal and external bleeding.

Vegetable Garden Path

HERBS SHOULD CERTAINLY FORM PART of any vegetable garden, be it a humble patch or a grand enclosure. Low-growing herbs need to be easy to pick, making them ideal for a pathside. Mix parsley, oregano, sage, and thyme with the smaller salad vegetables in the garden and on the table – nothing beats a fresh salad with aromatic herb leaves.

Gardener's Notes

Some of the many small culinary herbs that grow well beside a path include parsley in its several forms, oregano (a herb that I use more than any other), chamomile, and looseleaf lettuce.

❧ SITE & SOIL Plant these herbs in rich, slightly alkaline, very well-drained soil in a sunny or lightly shaded position.

❧ PLANT CARE Grow parsley as annual and water well. Harvest, then dry chamomile flowers throughout summer.

CRISPY PARSLEY
Petroselinum crispum
Attractive, and having a gentle flavor, parsley is used mostly to garnish food. It is also good if made into soup, or as the major ingredient in a salad.

FRENCH MARJORAM
Origanum onites
All the sunshine of the Mediterranean appears to be packed into this culinary herb. Sweeter and more perfumed than *O. vulgare*, this and *O. majorana* are delicious in salads and with apples and pears.

WELL-ORDERED ENCLOSURE

A path alongside this vegetable garden is edged with catmint, Nepeta racemosa, *and boxwood,* Buxus sempervirens. *Beyond, lined up with the greenhouse, are ranks of lettuce, onions, beans, and artichokes.*

CHAMOMILE
Chamaemelum nobile
Fragrant leaves and flowers have a clean, slightly applelike scent. The dried flower heads and young leaves make a calming and sleep-inducing infusion. •

FRENCH PARSLEY
Petroselinum crispum var. *neapolitanum*
Flat-leaved parsley has a strong, celery-like taste in • salads and cooking. An infusion revives the appetite.

LOOSELEAF LETTUCE
Lactuca sativa 'Lollo Rossa'
Eat the slightly bitter leaves of this curly bronze-leaved endive as soon as possible, once picked. •

Colorful Low Life

BESIDE THE PATH IN SUMMER, I like to have herbs that are both aromatic and attractive. At this time when the garden is in full bloom, their flowers are an added bonus. Later, in autumn, not as many plants are available to create a decorative foreground. Happily, this is when many heathers and ornamental cabbages come into their own.

PINK AND SILVER CARPET

Low-growing Origanum laevigatum *has highly aromatic leaves and deep pink flowers on red stems. It looks very striking in combination with the aromatic metallic-silver leaves of* Artemisia 'Powis Castle'.

SPICY AROMA

This basil, Ocimum basilicum *'Cinnamon', has strongly scented leaves. Behind it in full flower is lemon bee balm,* Monarda citriodora, *a native of North America, where the plant is used as a tea flavoring.*

ORANGE-SCENTED CHAMELEON

The leaves of Houttuynia cordata *'Chameleon' have incredible red, yellow, and green variegations. Strongly scented of bitter orange peel, they are used to flavor oriental dishes. The plant prefers a damp site.*

Gardener's Notes

This showy autumnal mix of heathers and decorative cabbages remains attractive through early spring in mild areas. The flowers of evergreen heather vary from red through purple and pink to white and gold. Most flower in late summer, autumn, and early winter.

❦ SITE & SOIL Give this group a sunny position with light, well-drained acid soil. Keep the heathers just moist as this replicates their natural habitat. Grow in groups of several plants for more dramatic impact.

❦ PLANT CARE Plant cabbages in autumn; they last all winter and tend to bolt in the spring. Until well established, keep the heathers well watered.

WINE-RED HEATHER
Calluna vulgaris 'Alexandra'
This strong dark color provides a good contrast to paler pink forms that predominate in this genus.

ORNAMENTAL CABBAGE
Brassica oleracea capitata
Many decorative cabbages now exist, with frilled or feathered leaves, in white, pink, purple, and green. As well as their culinary uses, cabbage leaves help relieve mastitis.

ICE-PINK HEATHER
Calluna vulgaris 'Cramond'
Heather cultivars all share the same herbal properties. Infuse the growing flowering shoots to make a tonic tea.

FRESH PINK HEATHER
Calluna vulgaris 'Darkness'
Heather plants improve the quality of the open ground where they grow and can be used for fuel. The flowering shoots yield a dye.

Fruiting Hedges

HAWTHORN, holly, euonymus, hazel, beech, wild rose, blackberry, and ivy are plants traditionally used for hedging. All have herbal uses, and all produce berries and fruits. Trimming the hedge is likely to cut down on the numbers of these fruits and berries, but there will always be enough to interest birds in the race to winter.

Gardener's Notes

While hawthorn is widely used for hedging, it is increasingly rare to see euonymus planted – a pity because the leaves turn maroon in autumn and its intriguing pink seed capsules contain orange seeds. Tree ivy is the mature growth of the common climbing ivy. It flowers profusely in autumn then produces black seeds in winter. Blackberries are unstoppable, but beautiful in flower and delicious in fruit.

❦ SITE & SOIL Grow such a hedge in sun or bright shade in any well-drained soil. Euonymus will not tolerate acid soil.

❦ PLANT CARE New hedges do not like competition from grass, so make sure it is removed until the hedge is established. Trim off main growth tips in the first year to promote a more bushy growth below.

BLACKBERRY
Rubus fruticosus
A fast-growing semi-evergreen climber with rich, black berries that are delicious raw or in jams, jellies, and preserves.

HAWTHORN
Crataegus laevigata
This small deciduous tree clips well to form an impenetrable summer hedge. Its red haws are used for heart problems and to regulate blood pressure.

IVY
Hedera helix
The evergreen leaves are toxic but are used nevertheless to treat whooping cough and bronchitis. Applied externally, they treat rheumatism, and, in a tincture, toothache.

GLOWING FIRETHORNS

The fiery colors of these evergreen pyracanthas, Pyracantha atalantioides *and* P. atalantioides *'Aurea',*
glitter brightly in the autumn sun. Together they form a dense thicket of stems and thorns.

EUONYMUS
Euonymus europaeus
The bark and roots of this tall
deciduous shrub treat liver
complaints. It is uscd externally
on wounds and abscesses. •

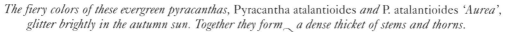

Winter Hedges

EVERGREENS GROWN AS HEDGES give form to the garden all year, but come into their own in winter, providing color when the landscape can be drab. Many have variegated, gold, and silver forms that give an impression of sunlight even on miserable days. Deciduous herbs add interest with seeds and a tracery of branches.

ENGLISH YEW •
Taxus baccata
A poisonous tree, sacred since the time of the druids, English yew was often planted in churchyards. Its very hard wood was used to make bows. Taxol from *T. brevifolia* now treats some cancers.

VARIEGATED HOLLY •
Ilex aquifolium
'Aureo-marginata'
Female plants bear bright red berries if pollinated by a male plant. It shares the medicinal qualities of *I. aquifolium* opposite.

Gardener's Notes

Yew, holly, and broom all add interesting shapes and textures to the winter garden. English yew and holly respond well to clipping, so are ideal candidates for hedges and topiary. Both also make shapely specimen trees and may reach 30ft (10m), but are slow growers. I particularly like holly clipped into a tight, small, tree shape. Broom is less controllable, but its fountain of green stems, to a height of around 6ft (2m), makes a dramatic statement toward the back of a border against a wall or hedge.

❧ SITE & PLANT English yew and holly grow in sun or semishade in a rich soil. Broom loves the sun and prefers soil that is less rich.

❧ PLANT CARE When they are young, give English yew and holly plenty of food to encourage good strong root systems. Trim them for topiary up to three times a year from midsummer to midautumn.

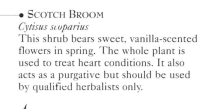

• SCOTCH BROOM
Cytisus scoparius
This shrub bears sweet, vanilla-scented flowers in spring. The whole plant is used to treat heart conditions. It also acts as a purgative but should be used by qualified herbalists only.

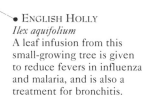

• ENGLISH HOLLY
Ilex aquifolium
A leaf infusion from this small-growing tree is given to reduce fevers in influenza and malaria, and is also a treatment for bronchitis.

FROSTED IVY

Many beautiful forms of Hedera helix exist. Here the foliage is frosted to further effect. Often underrated, this evergreen self-clinging climber will grow through hedges or carpet the ground beside shady paths.

SWEET CHESTNUTS

The prickly seed capsules of the sweet chestnut, Castanea sativa, drop with its leaves in autumn and open to reveal their chunky nuts. These treat coughs and are delicious roasted, candied, or made into stuffings.

CONTAINERS

THE GREAT ADVANTAGE of growing herbs in containers is that you can give them exactly the right conditions, by controlling soil type, drainage, and position. This enables you to grow favorites that might otherwise not suit your garden, and in return they should reward you with a wondrous show of leaves and flowers.

Pots and tubs are an ideal way to draw attention to the more decorative herbs such as French marigolds, nasturtiums, lilies, scented geraniums, rosemary, and thyme. Quite a few culinary herbs, especially Mediterranean ones, thrive in very well-drained soil and weather conditions that are not too cold or wet. This makes them ideal for pot-culture: there they can have good drainage, and can be moved to a more favorable site once the weather cools. A sunny place that is frost free, but not hot, is usually

ideal; perhaps a garden shed or greenhouse with the possibility of occasional artificial heating in severe weather. If containers are not too large, move them around from one position to another for variety throughout the growing season.

In gardens that have an abundance of space, don't restrict yourself to small pots. Make a feature of shrubs and even trees by having one specimen per pot. Larger containers, however, can be back-breaking, so if you want to grow herbs such as birch, juniper, fig, privet,

holly, or yew in containers, decide on a permanent spot for your choice. For those with limited space or no garden at all, pots offer the opportunity to grow herbs on a window sill or tiny patio.

Containers dry out very quickly, particularly in hot summer's weather, when you may have to water twice a day. Even when it rains, the roots in containers may not receive enough water. In winter, pots need occasional watering to keep the soil just moist, though never in icy weather.

△ ESSENCE OF PEPPERMINT
In a shady position, a pot spilling over with Corsican mint, Mentha requienii, *is well set off against a background of hosta leaves.*

◁ SILVERY PINK SALUTE
A weathered terra-cotta pot packed with silver-pink Scots heather makes a wonderful autumn show against an old kitchen door.

BRIGHT AS A BERRY ▷
The leaves and berries of evergreen firethorn and wintergreen shine forth during autumn when most color has gone from the garden.

Mediterranean Medley

A HIGH PROPORTION OF EDIBLE HERBS are frost tender and need
to be protected from an excess of cold and moisture. It is usually
a combination of these two factors that kills plants. Thus it is with
the citrus, pomegranate, and geranium seen here. Grown in pots,
they can be moved to a more favorable spot for the winter.

SAGE
Salvia officinalis
Use small quantities in
cooking – particularly as
a flavoring for pork and
liver. An infusion aids
the digestion and serves
to reduce fevers.

POMEGRANATE
Punica granatum
Grenadine, a cordial made
from pomegranate juice, is
delicious in ices, sorbets,
daiquiri cocktails, and
punches. The root bark
combats tapeworms
effectively.

PARADE OF CITRUS

*Citrus love to be outside all summer; in winter they tolerate a little
frost, but dislike a mix of cold and wet. Citrus fruits are packed with
vitamin C; their flowers and leaves are used in cosmetics and perfumes.*

POTTED THYME

*Thymes enjoy very well-drained soil, so they do well in pots where
drainage is better. In cold, damp areas, they can be given winter shelter.
This pot of* Thymus x citriodorus *sits happily beside a gravel path.*

STANDARD ROSEMARY
Rosmarinus officinalis
Cook it with lamb and pork. Medicinally, it is used for a number of anxiety-related illnesses and to improve circulation. •

SCENTED GERANIUM
Pelargonium 'Radula'
Its scent is sharper and more aromatic than 'Graveolens'. Use the fresh leaves in sorbets; dry them to add to potpourri. They are also a perfume ingredient. •

Gardener's Notes

This group of herbs in pots is wonderfully aromatic. Sage and rosemary are from the Mediterranean, scented geraniums are South African, and the pomegranate comes from the Middle East. All enjoy similar conditions, however: good drainage and sunlight.

❧ SITE & SOIL Pot in very well-drained, medium-rich soil, and place in a sunny spot in summer. In winter, shelter pomegranates and geraniums where it is light and frost free.

❧ PLANT CARE Take geranium cuttings in late summer; replace old plants after two years. To train the rosemary into a standard, grow one leader, removing side shoots until the required height is reached, then allow shoots to develop.

• **ROSE GERANIUM**
Pelargonium 'Graveolens'
The fresh rose-scented leaves can be infused to make a digestive tea. Oil is used in skin-care products. It bears pale pink flowers.

Bitter Sweet

THE DIFFERENCES IN APPEARANCE between one herb and another is
a constant source of amazement to me. Interestingly, many herbs
sweet in flavor, such as violets and pansies, are delicate in form,
while plants such as spiky juniper and agave have bitter properties.
Explore and contrast these variations for rewarding results.

VIOLETS
Viola 'Blueberry Cream'
A floriferous pansy, ideal for sugared
flowers. Paint the petals with egg
white, and dust them with sugar.

IVY-LEAVED VIOLET
Viola hederacea
This violet has similar properties to
those of *V. odorata*, and its oil is used in
perfumery. Herbalist Gerard says of a
sugared violet "especially it comforteth
the heart and other inward parts."

Gardener's Notes

Here is an intriguing potted mix of bitter and sweet. The viola family, and in particular violets, have a highly individual perfume and sweet-tasting flower petals. The reverse is true of common juniper, which has pungent leaves and bitter berrylike cones. Other junipers have poisonous oils. In containers, always grow one of the dwarf varieties.

❦ SITE & SOIL Junipers are unfussy growers, so give them what the violas like: a moist but well-drained soil in sun or semishade. The violets may need some protection in winter.

❦ PLANT CARE Remove violet flowers as soon as they die – this will promote new flowering growth. Clip the juniper to control its growth. When juniper roots start to take over the pot, transfer the plants to the garden.

WILD PANSY BASKET

Wild pansy or heartsease, Viola tricolor, *makes a wonderful subject for a hanging basket, seen here against the ancient trunk of a fig tree. It flowers from late spring until autumn if the dead flowers are removed.*

• JUNIPER TREE
Juniperus squamata
'Blue Carpet'
Like many other junipers, this cultivar has toxic resin and the foliage can cause an allergic reaction. The leaves and twigs are burned in some Indian temples.

BEAUTY AND THE BEAST

Potted geraniums contrast with prickly Agave americana *'Variegata', which, although it is a relatively hardy succulent, will need protection from winter cold and wet. Fibers in its leaves are used to make rope.*

Tender Exotics

MANY TROPICAL HERBS have attractive flowers and foliage that need year-round warmth to survive. The group I have chosen will survive winter temperatures only down to 37°F (3°C), with the exception of dwarf mountain pine. In cooler climates grow these attractive herbs in pots and move them for winter protection.

DEADLY BUT BEAUTIFUL

The beauty of the glory lily, Gloriosa superba *'Rothschildiana', belies its potency: its sap was used to poison arrow tips. Tiny quantities of the sap are given in the treatment of leprosy.*

BAUBLES OF SUNSHINE

This mimosa, Acacia dealbata, *makes an excellent, floriferous potted plant, and it will withstand a little frost. The bark, rich in tannin, yields a gum. Its flowers and young shoots are edible when cooked.*

Gardener's Notes

A disparate but attractive group of plants. Grown in glazed jars they look equally impressive in a cool conservatory or light airy room over winter, or in a sheltered spot outside over summer.

❦ SITE & SOIL All need well-drained soil, with many shards in the bottom of the pots. Pines require an acid potting soil. Inside, place where it is light out of direct sunlight; outside, in light sun or dappled shade.

❦ PLANT CARE Keep soil just moist all year and feed every two weeks in summer with a weak multipurpose liquid fertilizer. In late spring repot the jasmine into a pot that is one size larger.

DWARF MOUNTAIN PINE ●
Pinus mugo var. *pumilio*
Oil, distilled from the needles, treats bronchial and respiratory problems. It is also used commercially in perfumes and bath products.

JASMINE
Jasminum polyanthum
Its fragrant late winter flowers can be dried and added to tea to make a refreshing infusion. Essential oil is used in perfumes. ●

LEMON
Citrus limon
Lemon peel and juice flavor both sweet and savory dishes and preserves. The juice treats congestion. Add the oil and peel to potpourri. ●

CALADOMIN
Citrus onites
This citrus grows well in pots, where it flowers and fruits freely. The small fruits make excellent preserves, especially when mixed with either limes or grapefruits. ●

AGAVE
Agave filifera
Leaf sap is used to lower fevers and for digestive problems. The fibers of the larger *A. americana*, which also grows extremely well in pots, are made into sisal. ●

A Range of Potted Delights

DECORATIVE HERBS make excellent specimens for pots. Culinary plants can be snipped for use in the kitchen; herbs with fragrant leaves should be placed where you can brush them as you walk by. All smaller or medium-sized herbs take to pots with relish, but they do need more care with watering than those in open ground.

FOUNTAIN OF GOLD AND SILVER

Rising from a lavender bed, an urn overflowing with bur marigold, Bidens tripartita, *and licorice plant,* Helichrysum petiolare, *is a splendid sight. "Eversilver" licorice spreads rapidly but is tender.*

HERBAL BENCH

A trough perched on a rustic old bench spills over with a mix of thymes. The nasturtiums, Tropaeolum majus, *alongside also make excellent potted plants, thriving in poor well-drained soil and plenty of sun.*

COOK'S BOUNTY

This window sill hosts a miniature herb garden. The lavender, parsley, variegated sage, basil, spignel, and thyme all make tasty additions to the cooking pot, but not so the bellflower, geranium, and ivy.

SCENTED ABUNDANCE

A terra-cotta bowl bulges with heliotrope, scented geraniums, and licorice plant. Feed this fragrant mix of plants with tomato fertilizer every two weeks throughout the summer to sustain an impressive show.

VARIEGATED GERANIUM
Pelargonium fragrans
'Variegatum'
The strong pine scent of
this geranium makes it
particularly effective as
bath salts and in aromatic
potpourris. •

VARIEGATED THYME •
Thymus 'Doone Valley'
This thyme has a lemon
flavor that works well with
fish and white meats. An
infusion aids digestion and
also improves coughs and
sore throats.

Gardener's Notes

Double-flowered balsam (not to be confused with
balsam poplar, *Populus balsamifera*) is mixed with sweet-
scented geraniums and variegated thyme in this oval
terra-cotta bowl with fruited swags. It would look very
attractive sitting on a window sill or a table on the patio.
❦ SITE & SOIL Plant in a moderately rich, well-drained
potting mix and display in a bright, not too sunny place.
❦ PLANT CARE Keep well watered but not soggy. Feed
every two weeks in summer with a multipurpose
fertilizer. Take cuttings of all plants in late summer, and
overwinter indoors. Plant out in early summer.

• ROSE BALSAM
Impatiens balsamina
Tom Thumb Series
Wild balsam has single
white or pink flowers, but
new strains such as these
with double flowers now
exist. The leaves can be
used as a poultice to treat
bruises and swollen joints.

SCENTED GERANIUM •
Pelargonium
'Prince of Orange'
The leaves exude a strong
orange scent when bruised.
Infuse with orange juice
and sugar syrup to make a
delicious sorbet. Use dried
leaves in potpourri.

Containers for Cooks

CULINARY HERBS IN CONTAINERS are useful and can be extremely decorative, too. The smaller species such as sage, thyme, marjoram, and basil are ideal, since their growth will not be too restricted by the size of the pot. Both watering and feeding are very important throughout the summer months since containers dry out quickly.

BEE BALM
Monarda didyma
Add the leaves to tea to make your own "Earl Grey" tea. An infusion improves the digestion. Both leaves and flowers are dried for potpourri. •

SPIGNEL •
Meum athamanticum
This is similar to dill *Anethum graveolens* but smaller. Its feathery leaves flavor oil for dressings and taste delicious in potato salad and fish dishes. An infusion helps mild digestive problems.

THYME •
Thymus vulgaris
'Silver Posie'
Used in bouquet garni, and in many Mediterranean dishes, thyme particularly complements the flavor of chicken, potatoes, and sautéed vegetables in cooking. It is expectorant and treats bronchitis, coughs, and congestion.

Gardener's Notes

A wire potato basket makes an ideal container for a group of culinary and decorative herbs. The basket may be lined with moss or, as it is here, with coconut fiber, then a layer of plastic.

❧ SITE & SOIL As with most herbs, these enjoy a sunny position in a rich well-drained potting mix. Make sure that you cut holes in the plastic so water can drain freely from the base of the container.

❧ PLANT CARE Wait until the plants are established before harvesting their leaves, and do not denude them too much. Water regularly – daily in hot dry weather – and feed weekly. Remove any flowers as they appear, to promote leaf growth.

• GERANIUM
Pelargonium crispum
'Variegatum'
The small crinkled leaves of this geranium have a peppery lemon smell and can be used to flavor desserts and ices, or dried to add to potpourri. They make a tea to aid digestion.

• PURPLE SAGE
Salvia officinalis
'Purpurascens'
This evergreen shares the properties of common sage. Its pungent leaves are eaten with pork, veal, and game. An infusion eases indigestion, sore throats, and mouth infections.

HERB JAR

A pot of culinary herbs, such as this one with French tarragon, wild strawberry, rosemary, mint, marjoram, and savory, in a sunny place near the kitchen door, will provide plenty of snippets for the cook.

SITTING PRETTY

The herb basket looks lovely sitting in a sunny spot against an ivy-clad wall, where it is fortunate to have a stone seat to itself. Leave a tiny gap for drainage between the basket base and the surface it is on.

Topiary in Containers

SEVERAL HERBS, such as bay, boxwood, English yew, privet, and rosemary, make excellent topiary subjects and thrive in pots where you can give them the right feeding, soil, watering, and position for their optimal enjoyment. Growing them in containers enables you to make occasional changes to the grouping.

GREEN PARTERRE

Pots always look splendid in a formal setting such as a boxwood-edged parterre; the large pots of sweetly scented tobacco, Nicotiana sylvestris, *seen here are certainly no exception. Grapefruit-scented* Cupressus macrocarpa *'Donard Gold', a strong astringent, makes a dramatic spiral centerpiece.*

Gardener's Notes

Boxwood, with its tiny evergreen leaves, is easily trained and clipped into complex but clean-edged topiary shapes; bay, with its larger leaves, is better as a mop-head, pyramid, cone, or pillar. Grow ivy or thyme around the base to cover the soil mix in the pots. Mop-heads are my favorite for standing on porches; domes or pyramids give a structured border to a bed of flowering plants or beside a path.

❧ SITE & SOIL Plant these in well-drained rich soil mix; they need it well-watered but not soggy. Boxwood will grow in either sun or shade. Bay prefers to be in sun or semishade.

❧ PLANT CARE Water lightly even in winter unless conditions are freezing. Fertilize once every two weeks during summer. Clip the boxwood and bay to encourage dense growth after shoots have hardened in summer. Take cuttings in late summer.

SPIRAL BOXWOOD •
Buxus sempervirens
This spiral evergreen boxwood is grown first as a pyramid, then cut into a thin spiral that can be developed as the plant grows. Boxwood was once used to treat toothache, but it is now grown mainly for edging and topiary in gardens. Commercially, its hard wood is used as an inlay.

TRIPLE-SPHERE BOXWOOD
Buxus sempervirens
Encourage side shoots to
produce base sphere. Remove
those immediately above to
give a bare stem, then repeat
the process to form the
• next two spheres.

BOXWOOD STANDARD
Buxus sempervirens
Remove all side shoots
and allow a long bare
stem to grow, before
promoting top growth
by encouraging the side
• shoots. Clip to shape.

BOXWOOD PYRAMID
Buxus sempervirens
'Handsworthensis'
A pyramid is the easiest
form to grow since it is
closest to the natural
• shape of the plant.

• **STANDARD BAY**
Laurus nobilis
A classic culinary
herb that can be
trimmed into
different shapes.
Remove all side
shoots from main
stem until plant
reaches the desired
height, then allow
to shoot out and
clip into a sphere.

THYME
Thymus vulgaris
'Silver Posie'
The variegated
leaves of this good
culinary thyme look
especially attractive
• in salads.

• **IVY**
Hedera helix 'Pedata'
All ivies are poisonous, although
in the 17th century extracts were
given for toothache and fevers.

PLANT DIRECTORY

MALCOLM HILLIER'S TOP 50 HERBS

THE TASK OF CHOOSING fifty special herbs that are attractive in the garden and of notable culinary, medicinal, or cosmetic use is not easy; there are enough contestants to fill an entire book. Those that follow are my favorites, with a few pointers to help you grow them and discover their potential. Sizes are approximate and information about uses is anecdotal.

HERBAL THOROUGHFARE
Rustic stone steps lead through this informal garden, providing a platform from which to enjoy the sights and scents of nearby herbs, and making access for harvest easy, too.

Achillea millefolium
YARROW

This perennial grows to around 24in (60cm) tall, has aromatic fernlike leaves, and small white or pink flower heads in summer. 'Cerise Queen' and 'Red Beauty' are color variants.

❦ CULTIVATION Easy to grow in most soils in sun. Plant seeds in spring, pot, then plant out in late autumn. Divide clumps in early spring, and cut back in autumn.
❦ USES A leaf infusion aids digestion and helps dispel colds. Infuse the flowers for a soothing bath; dry them for decoration.

Allium schoenoprasum
CHIVES

Low-growing and tussock-forming with pink summer flowers, this 9in- (22cm-) tall edible bulb is a good edging plant. Other edible alliums include garlic (*A. sativus*) and onion (*A. cepa*).

❦ CULTIVATION Chives grow in any well-drained soil in sun or semishade. Plant seeds out in spring; divide clumps every three years, either in spring or autumn.
❦ USES Fresh leaves and flowers are a mild aid to digestion; use in salads or hot dishes. Plants keep aphids at bay in the garden.

Aloysia triphylla
LEMON VERBENA

A deciduous shrub, grown as an annual in cold areas. Its leaves are intensely lemon-scented, so plant where passers-by will brush them. Up to 6ft (2m) tall, it bears tiny white summer flowers.

❧ CULTIVATION Best grown in a sheltered, sunny position. Plant seeds in late spring. Take cuttings in midsummer, protect from frost in winter, and plant out in late spring.

❧ USES Make a refreshing infusion from the leaves; use to flavor custards and sorbets. Dry the leaves to add to potpourris.

Angelica archangelica
ANGELICA

This perennial, which can reach 8ft (2.5m), is best grown as a biennial; if the seed heads that follow its flowers are not removed, the plant dies. Stems, leaves, and seeds are sweetly aromatic.

❧ CULTIVATION Plant in moist, rich soils in sun or semishade. Sow seeds in spring for flowers the following year. Self-seeds freely. Trim spent flower heads.

❧ USES A leaf infusion benefits digestive problems. Tender young stems can be candied. Dried seed heads are decorative.

Artemisia abrotanum
SOUTHERNWOOD

The feathery silver-green leaves of this 3ft- (1m-) high, hardy evergreen shrub have a tangy-sweet fragrance when brushed against, so plant it next to a path, perhaps as a low hedge.

❧ CULTIVATION Grow in well-drained soil in sun. Remove its coarse yellow flowers as they appear. Take semiripe cuttings in late summer; plant out the following autumn.

❧ USES Plants in the garden keep pests at bay; sachets of dried leaves repel moths. An infusion is antiseptic and a good insecticide.

Anethum graveolens
DILL

A fast-growing annual that reaches a height of 3ft (1m). Its single stem carries fine, aromatic gray-green leaves and umbels of golden green summer flowers. Edible seeds follow.

❧ CULTIVATION Grow in any well-drained soil in sun. Sow seeds from spring onward; the plants will be ready two months later.

❧ USES Dill is delicious eaten with fish and white poultry. Seeds can be dried or deep frozen and are particularly flavorful. Drink an infusion for digestive problems.

Anthriscus cerefolium
CHERVIL

Small umbels of insignificant white flowers top this 18in- (45cm-) tall annual from spring into summer. It slightly resembles cow-parsley, with its flowers and feathery light green leaves.

❧ CULTIVATION Likes most well-drained soils in semishade. Harvest when leaves and stems are young, so more will grow.

❧ USES Delicious in salads and as *fines herbes* with egg dishes, white meat, and fish, but too much cooking destroys its delicate flavor. An infusion is a good restorative.

Artemisia dracunculus
TARRAGON

About 18in (45cm) tall, this perennial is best planted near the front of the herb border or in pots – its unique flavor more than compensates for its straggly, somewhat spindly appearance.

❧ CULTIVATION Prefers very well-drained soil in sun. Divide in spring. Trim any leggy growth for culinary use as necessary. Move pots to a cool, light position inside in winter.

❧ USES Leaves retain their flavor when frozen or dried, are good with chicken and egg dishes, and, in small quantities, fish.

Betula pendula
SILVER BIRCH

The shimmering deciduous leaves of this beautiful, silver-barked tree cast only a light shade. Growing to 70ft (20m) tall, the trees look particularly attractive grown in a group or copse.

🌿 CULTIVATION Plant young specimens in winter when the ground is not frozen or, in cooler areas, in spring. They enjoy a moist, but well-drained neutral to acid soil in sun.
🌿 USES An infusion of young leaves relieves rheumatism; it is also antiseptic. Added to soap, the bud oil helps clear skin problems.

Borago officinalis
BORAGE

This annual is an attractive border plant growing to 3ft (1m) tall. It bears wondrous, nodding blue flowers, which, like the leaves, have a mild cucumber flavor. It self-seeds readily.

🌿 CULTIVATION Plant in sun or semishade in spring, in any well-drained soil. Remove all unwanted seedlings. White- and pink-flowered variations are also available.
🌿 USES Add leaves and flowers to salads. Float in summer cocktails or white wine punch. Young shoots can be steamed as a vegetable.

Buxus sempervirens
BOXWOOD

A traditional evergreen hedging, this shrub or small tree, up to 15ft (5m) tall, has leaves that give off a foxy scent, particularly when damp. For low edging 'Suffruticosa' is the best form.

🌿 CULTIVATION Tolerant of sun or semi-shade, it is best planted in spring in any well-drained soil. For hedging, plant 12in (30cm) apart. Take cuttings in late summer.
🌿 USES Boxwood is excellent for topiary. Leaves and bark are toxic, but are used in homeopathy to treat rheumatism.

Calendula officinalis
POT MARIGOLD

All parts of this long-flowering annual are tangy and aromatic. It has orange or yellow daisylike flowers throughout summer and autumn. The plant grows to a height of 20in (50cm).

🌿 CULTIVATION Grow in any well-drained soil. Plant seeds where you want them to grow, in the middle of spring. Deadhead for prolonged flower production. Self-seeds.
🌿 USES Petals can be used as food dye. Add these and young leaves to salads. Oil is used in shampoos and treats skin disorders.

Chamaemelum nobile
CHAMOMILE

This low-spreading, sweetly aromatic, 6in- (15cm-) tall perennial is ideal for planting between paving stones. 'Treneague' produces no flowers and is therefore excellent for making a lawn.

🌿 CULTIVATION Grows in any well-drained soil in sun. Plant 6in (15cm) apart in spring for a lawn or seat, although it will not withstand too much wear and tear.
🌿 USES Infuse flowers, fresh or dried, for a soothing, relaxing drink. Use in potpourri, especially in cushions and sachets.

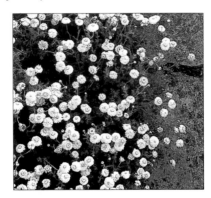

Cichorium intybus
CHICORY

The growth of this perennial, to 4ft (1.2m), tall is straggly, but it bears lovely blue summer flowers. The hearts, or chicons, of its leaves are "forced" to produce salad in winter.

🌿 CULTIVATION For decorative purposes, grow in rich, well-drained soil in sun. For salads, lift the roots in late autumn, plant in sand, and force in a warm dark place.
🌿 USES Eat as a salad or vegetable. Add ground root to coffee to make it less of a stimulant. Root infusion benefits digestion.

Coriandrum sativum
CILANTRO/CORIANDER

This intensely aromatic tender annual grows to 24in (60cm). Its leaves resemble flat parsley, and these and all parts, including the seeds, lend an acquired "metallic" flavor to food.

❦ CULTIVATION Seeds sown in late spring will mature and produce seed by autumn. Grow in sun in rich, well-drained soil.
❦ USES A favored flavoring for many meat and fish dishes, particularly in Middle Eastern and Southeast Asian dishes. Both leaves and seeds act as a digestive.

Digitalis purpurea
FOXGLOVE

A stately biennial with a tall flower spire, to 6ft (2m) high. Tubular, lipped flowers with spotted throats are produced in early summer. Ideal grown in groups at the back of a border.

❦ CULTIVATION Prefers moist, well-drained acid soil in semishade. Sow seeds in spring for flowers the following year. Remove any dead spikes to encourage further flowering.
❦ USES This poisonous plant contains Digitalin, which is used in the treatment of heart disease. *D. lanata* is more potent.

Foeniculum vulgare
FENNEL

All parts of this short-lived perennial have a strong anise aroma. At 5ft (1.5m) tall, fennel is elegant with feathery plumes of leaves and umbels of golden green flowers in summer.

❦ CULTIVATION Plant seeds in early spring; harvest the leaves all through summer and the seeds in autumn. The purple-leaved form is an attractive alternative.
❦ USES Leaves flavor salads, meat, and fish dishes – including curries and oriental dishes. Dried seeds retain their flavor.

Crocus sativus
SAFFRON

Long, hot summers are needed to coax this pretty 6in- (15cm-) tall bulb into plentiful flower in autumn. The flavor and color of its stigmas (only three per flower) have been valued for centuries.

❦ CULTIVATION Bulbs need as much sun as possible in a rich, well-drained soil. Feed with a potash fertilizer from early summer.
❦ USES Saffron is extremely expensive, but very small quantities are delicious with rice, fish, and white meat dishes, to which it will also lend a beautiful, rich golden color.

Eruca vesicaria subsp. *sativa*
ARUGULA

Of little decorative merit, this fast-growing annual is grown for its tangy young leaves. Growing to about 30in (75cm) in six weeks, it produces little white flowers, then goes to seed.

❦ CULTIVATION Arugula prefers a semi-shaded position in a rich, well-drained soil. Sow seeds in succession from the middle of spring for several crops through summer.
❦ USES Delicious added to salads – older leaves have a stronger flavor. In the past, an infusion was used as a cough mixture.

Galium odoratum
SWEET WOODRUFF

This attractive low-growing perennial – to around 6in- (15cm-) tall – produces tiny, starry white flowers in late spring above a thick groundcover of rufflike whorls of rich green leaves.

❦ CULTIVATION Grow in well-drained, but moist alkaline soil in light shade. Sow seeds or divide existing plants in spring.
❦ USES The dried young leaves make a refreshing infusion, which aids digestion. A haylike aroma develops as leaves dry – use to scent potpourris for sachets or cushions.

Hyssopus officinalis
HYSSOP

Hyssop, a semievergreen shrub, growing to 18in (45cm) tall, makes an attractive edging plant. Aromatic and mound-forming, it produces spires of purple-blue flowers in late summer.

❦ CULTIVATION Grow in well-drained soil in a sunny site. Sow seeds in spring, plant out in autumn. Take cuttings in early summer.
❦ USES Add the sagey mint-flavored leaves to soups, meat dishes, and, with flowers, to salads. Medicinally, the leaves contain antiseptic and antiviral oils and treat bruises.

Iris germanica 'Florentina'
ORRIS

Plant this beautiful, sweet-scented iris at the front of a border, since it only grows to 24in (60cm) in height. When dried, its rhizomes have a perfume like that of violets. The plant is poisonous.

❦ CULTIVATION Choose a very well-drained sunny position. Plant the rhizomes so that their tops are level with the soil. Divide the rhizomes every third year after flowering.
❦ USES Grind dry rhizomes to a powder to use as a fixative in potpourris – it also adds a violet scent. Was once used as a purgative.

Laurus nobilis
BAY

This evergreen tree, which can reach 30ft (10m) in height, is often grown as a topiary shrub and is excellent in containers. Shelter it from frost and cold in areas with hard winters.

❦ CULTIVATION Thrives in well-drained soil in sun or light shade. Make sure soil in pots is kept lightly watered even during winter. Good grown as a hedge in mild areas.
❦ USES Aromatic leaves give a distinctive flavor in bouquet garni, soups, stews, and stock. Also good with savory or sweet rice.

Inula helenium
ELECAMPANE

This 8ft (2.5m) tall perennial with yellow daisylike flowers makes a strong decorative statement at the back of a border, especially mixed with other yellow- and orange-flowered herbs.

❦ CULTIVATION Grow in a sunny position in well-drained soil. The rhizomatous root system can be split in late spring. Cut back in autumn to prevent profuse self-seeding.
❦ USES Cook or dry the banana-scented rhizomes. Roots are candied; a root infusion treats coughs. Dry flowers for decoration.

Juniperus communis
COMMON JUNIPER

There are several garden forms, both upright and spreading, of this aromatic, evergreen conifer, which grows wild as a shrub or small tree. Its berrylike cones are rich in fragrant oil.

❦ CULTIVATION Prefers well-drained soil in sun or light shade. Seeds ripen in autumn. Grow plants in a pot for two years before planting out. Trim to maintain shape.
❦ USES Add two crushed berries to strong meats and game. The berries are also used to flavor gin. Oil treats acne and eczema.

Lavandula angustifolia
LAVENDER

Lavender, the classic cottage-garden herb, is a 3ft- (1m-) tall, mounding, evergreen shrub. Flower spikes top aromatic leaves in summer. It is wonderful grown as an informal hedge.

❦ CULTIVATION A Mediterranean plant, it needs well-drained soil and a sunny site. Overwinter cuttings taken in late summer in a cold frame, and plant out in late spring.
❦ USES Mostly used in perfumery and potpourri, it also flavors ice cream or tarts. An infusion aids digestion; the oil is antiseptic.

Levisticum officinale
LOVAGE

A long-lived perennial, which, at 6ft (2m) tall, is ideal for the back of the border. Its flowers, similar to those of fennel, appear in midsummer above attractive, celery-flavored leaves.

❦ CULTIVATION Grow in moist but well-drained soil in a sunny position. Cut back before flowering to produce a new set of young shoots. Divide clumps in late spring.
❦ USES Young leaves are fragrant in salads, soups, and in fish sauces. Syrup made from the root acts as an expectorant.

Lilium candidum
MADONNA LILY

A lovely lily with several shining white flowers on a 4ft- (1.2m-) tall stem. It has a beautiful scent that is sweet, fresh, and not cloying. Since early times, it has been a symbol of purity.

❦ CULTIVATION Unlike most other lilies, it should not be planted too deeply. Best in a sunny site in groups or pots. Dust the bulbs with fungicide powder before planting.
❦ USES The edible bulbs contain a juice that benefits a variety of skin problems, while the flowers are used in perfumery.

Melissa officinalis
LEMON BALM

Plant this 3ft- (1m-) tall, lemon-scented perennial where its pretty scallop-edged leaves can be brushed against. Variegated *M. officinalis* 'Variegata' has most attractive leaves.

❦ CULTIVATION Lemon balm requires well-drained soil in sun or semishade. Divide clumps in spring or autumn. Remove the insignificant flowers to encourage foliage.
❦ USES An infusion made from the leaves is delicious and aids sleep. The leaves are also used to flavor ice creams and custards.

Mentha suaveolens
APPLE MINT

The rounded, hairy leaves of this mint last till the end of autumn. About 12in (30cm) high, it is good for pots or mixed plantings at the front of a border. 'Variegata' has cream-edged leaves.

❦ CULTIVATION Plant in moist but well-drained soil in sun or semishade. Propagate by layering. Like most mints, it is invasive, so plant in a bottomless pot in the ground.
❦ USES The apple flavor is delicious with new potatoes, lamb dishes, and tzatziki; the leaves decorate many desserts and drinks.

Monarda didyma
BEE BALM

Hybrids of this 3ft- (1m-) tall perennial bear pretty summer flowers that are red, pink, white, or lilac. Plant in the middle of a border or along a path, where you can enjoy its leaf scent.

❦ CULTIVATION Prefers sun or semishade in moist but well-drained soil. Divide plants every third year. Harvest young leaves for drying before flowers appear.
❦ USES Dry the spicy-sweet leaves to make a refreshing infusion. When mixed with tea leaves, it makes "Earl Grey" tea.

Myrrhis odorata
SWEET CICELY

Usually grown as an annual, this perennial reaches a height of 6ft (2m). With ferny leaves and umbels of white summer flowers, it makes an attractive addition to the back of a border.

❦ CULTIVATION Plant seeds in succession in spring to ensure a good supply of the fresh young leaves. Thrives in sun or semishade in rich, moist but well-drained soil.
❦ USES Add its delicately sweet-spicy leaves and young green seeds to salads. Delicious in sauces for fish or in omelettes.

Ocimum basilicum
BASIL

Basil is an annual that is highly susceptible to cold, so may be best in pots. Its strongly aromatic leaves freeze well but loose their flavor when dried. Plants grow to about 24in (60cm) tall.

❦ CULTIVATION Needs light, well-drained soil in full sun. Plant seeds inside in early spring – young plants should not be placed outside until the summer is quite warm.
❦ USES Flavors Mediterranean dishes. It is a main ingredient for pesto and is good in salads. An infusion settles the stomach.

Origanum vulgare
OREGANO

Redolent of the Mediterranean, this perennial with aromatic leaves grows to 24in (60cm) tall. Leaves retain good flavor when dried or frozen. *O. majorana* (marjoram) is similar.

❦ CULTIVATION Plant in late spring in any well-drained soil in a sunny position. Take softwood cuttings in late spring.
❦ USES A delicious culinary herb for many dishes, particularly pork and veal recipes and, of course, pizzas. Use fresh leaves in salads. Dry flowers for decoration.

Pelargonium capitatum
ROSE GERANIUM

This rose-scented subshrub grows to a height of 18in (45cm). Other scented species include *P. crispum* – orange, *P. radens* – lemon, *P. tomentosum* – mint, and *P. odoratissimum* – apple.

❦ CULTIVATION Plant in light, well-drained soil in sun. Take cuttings in late summer, and overwinter in a frost-free site.
❦ USES Dried leaves are delicious in pot-pourri. Leaf infusions are good for preserves and ice creams. The volatile oil is used in perfumes, soaps, and shampoos.

Petroselinum crispum
PARSLEY

An attractive 18in- (45cm-) tall biennial best grown as an annual. Use as edging to a path, or plant in a group at the front of a border. Different forms have more and less divided leaves.

❦ CULTIVATION Sow seeds from early spring where they are to grow, in rich, moist but well-drained soil in sun or semishade.
❦ USES Leaves are slightly bitter, but tasty in salads or scattered on vegetable, meat, or fish dishes. I like the flavor of flat-leaved French or Italian parsley (var. *neapolitanum*).

Phlomis fruticosa
JERUSALEM SAGE

The decorative leaves of this evergreen shrub are silver-felted. It grows to 3ft (1m) in height. Golden yellow flowers (pink for *P. italica*) in whorls are produced in high summer.

❦ CULTIVATION Grow in sun in a light, well-drained soil. Remove leggy growths to keep in good shape. Propagate by layering or taking cuttings in late summer.
❦ USES The aromatic leaves are made into a refreshing infusion. Air-dry the flowering stems for use in decorative displays.

Rosa rugosa 'Alba'
RUGOSA ROSE

With its healthy, dark green leaves, highly scented white summer flowers, and tomato-like hips, this 5ft- (1.5m-) tall shrub is an excellent plant. Grow with other rugosas as a hedge.

❦ CULTIVATION Plant container-grown roses in early winter in warmer areas, otherwise plant in spring. Prefers rich, well-drained soil in sun. Feed regularly through summer.
❦ USES Add petals to salads or, crystallized, to desserts. A petal infusion makes rose water, and the vitamin C-rich hips, a syrup.

Rosmarinus officinalis
ROSEMARY

Site this 4ft- (1.2m-) tall, highly aromatic, evergreen shrub where its fine leaves can be brushed against to release their fragrance. Silvery blue flowers last from winter through spring.

❦ CULTIVATION This Mediterranean herb prefers sun and well-drained soil. In colder areas, choose a sheltered site. Take semi-ripe cuttings in summer.
❦ USES The strong, heady flavor is very good with lamb, pork, and in apple pie. It was thought to improve sight and memory.

Rumex acetosa
SORREL

As its Latin name implies, this spinach-like 24in- (60cm-) tall perennial has acid-tasting leaves. Regular picking ensures a succession of young leaves from spring through to autumn.

❦ CULTIVATION Sorrel grows in any well-drained soil in sun or semishade. Pick the leaves often, and remove flowering stems as they appear to encourage new growth.
❦ USES Delicious as a salad herb, or to make a lemon-flavored soup. Make use of its sharpness to enhance green sauces.

Ruta graveolens
RUE

This feathery silver-blue perennial is effective at the front of a border and makes an extremely decorative low hedge, around 24in (60cm) in height. Yellow flowers appear in midsummer.

❦ CULTIVATION Plant in winter or spring in any well-drained, sunny soil. Clip to keep neat. Leaves may cause an allergic reaction. 'Jackman's Blue' has very blue-silver leaves.
❦ USES Leaves were once carried to keep the plague at bay and repel insects. Include tiny quantities in sauces for meat and fish.

Salvia officinalis
SAGE

This aromatic shrub has gray-green, evergreen, textured leaves. Decorative forms such as 'Icterina' and 'Purpurascens' have the same culinary properties as common sage.

❦ CULTIVATION Grow in good well-drained alkaline soil in full sun. Take cuttings or layer stems in late summer.
❦ USES Particularly good with pork and game and in stuffings and sausages. Also delicious with liver. A leaf infusion benefits sore throats and tickly coughs.

Sambucus nigra
ELDER

A beautiful, deciduous, tall shrub or small tree that grows to a height of 15ft (5m), with large, flat heads of scented white flowers in summer followed by black berries.

❦ CULTIVATION Grow in any well-drained soil. Remove rampant self-sown seedlings.
❦ USES The fragrant flowers can be used to make wine and cordial or flavor fruits and jams. A flower infusion benefits eyes. The berries, high in vitamin C, are made into pies or conserves.

Santolina chamaecyparissus
LAVENDER COTTON

A sharp-scented evergreen perennial, with silvery filigree leaves and coarse yellow summer flowers. Growing to 24in (60cm) high, it makes a good edging or filler between low hedgings.

❦ CULTIVATION Grow in well-drained sandy soil in sun. Take cuttings in late summer. Remove flowers when they appear, to encourage healthy growth of scented leaves.
❦ USES The dried leaves can be used in potpourris or in sachets to repel moths. It was used in medieval times to treat worms.

FEVERFEW
Tanacetum parthenium

Aromatic, fernlike leaves and white daisy flowers cover this perennial in summer. 24in (60cm) tall, it is ideal for the front of the border or as edging. *T. parthenium* 'Aureum' has gold leaves.

❧ CULTIVATION Grow in any well-drained soil in sun. Plants self-seed freely. Divide clumps in late autumn or spring.
❧ USES Place dried flowers and leaves in sachets to repel moths. Leaf infusions are taken to relieve insomnia, soothe headaches (particularly migraines), and reduce fever.

TANSY
Tanacetum vulgare

Strongly bitter with aromatic leaves, this perennial grows to a height of 4ft (1.2m). It has feathery, toothed green leaves and yellow button flowers in summer. Rootstock can be invasive.

❧ CULTIVATION Grow in dry soil in sun or semishade in containers, so that it cannot spread. Remove brown flower heads.
❧ USES Leaves are a good insect repellent. Small amounts of the tonic and stimulant leaves were added to cakes after fasting in Lent, but they may be toxic if eaten.

GERMANDER
Teucrium chamaedrys

Excellent as an edging or a solid filler in a parterre, this subshrub grows to around 18in (45cm) tall. It has aromatic, toothed evergreen leaves and pinkish flowers in late summer.

❧ CULTIVATION Grow in any well-drained soil in a sunny site. Divide in spring, take cuttings in early summer, or layer shoots.
❧ USES The leaves are used commercially to flavor vermouth. An infusion of the leaves is expectorant and also antiseptic, but long-term use may damage the liver.

THYME
Thymus serpyllum 'Lemon Curd'

Low-growing to a height of 3in (7cm), this evergreen subshrub thrives beside paths or in paving cracks. Both its leaves and lilac-pink summer flowers have a lemon fragrance.

❧ CULTIVATION All thymes require a very well-drained soil in a sunny position. Take cuttings in midsummer, plant out in winter in milder areas, elsewhere plant in spring.
❧ USES Added to many savory dishes, particularly poultry. Use in bouquet garni. Infusions aid indigestion and are antiseptic.

NASTURTIUM
Tropaeolum majus

This highly decorative annual clambers to 6ft (2m) or more. Scented red, pink, orange, or yellow flowers appear through summer and autumn. Grow in containers, as edging, or over a wall.

❧ CULTIVATION Plant seeds in spring, in well-drained sunny soil that is not too rich. Thin as necessary. Plants are particularly susceptible to black fly attack.
❧ USES Flowers, leaves, and seeds are delicious in salads with their sweet peppery taste, which resembles that of watercress.

SWEET VIOLET
Viola odorata

This small perennial is blessed with a most beautiful perfume and bears its edible flowers in early spring. Violas produce flowers in most seasons of the year, and many are perfumed.

❧ CULTIVATION Best planted in a partially shade site in a rich, moist but well-drained soil. Cuttings can be taken in midsummer.
❧ USES Both flowers and leaves are used in perfumery. They can treat coughs and bronchitis. In the kitchen add to salads or crystallize flowers to decorate desserts.

HERBS FOR SPECIFIC USES

It can be hard selecting herbs to grow in the garden or in pots. Here are my suggestions for certain sites, situations, and uses. I hope they will assist you to choose the herbs that most closely meet your requirements.

HERBS FOR DRYING

Anethum graveolens
Artemisia dracunculus
Coriandrum sativum (seeds)
Crocus sativus
Foeniculum vulgare (seeds)
Juniperus communis (berries)
Laurus nobilis
Origanum species
Rosmarinus officinalis
Salvia officinalis
Thymus species

HERBS FOR FREEZING

Allium schoenoprasm
Anthriscus cerefolium
Artemisia dracunculus
Coriandrum sativum
Melissa officinalis
Mentha species
Myrrhis odorata
Ocimum basilicum
Petroselinum crispum
Satureja species
Rumex acetosa

HERBS FOR CUTTING

Alchemilla vulgaris
Anethum graveolens
Calendula officinalis
Dianthus species
Digitalis species
Erysimum species
Lilium candidum
Lupinus polyphyllus
Matthiola species
Monarda didyma
Nigella damascena
Paeonia species
Rosa species

HERBS FOR HEDGES

Buxus sempervirens
Elaeagnus species
Crataegus species
Hedera species
Ilex species
Ligustrum species
Prunus laurocerasus
Satureja species
Taxus species

HERBS FOR COLOR

Acacia dealbata
Achillea millefolium
Alcea rosea
Asclepias tuberosa
Chrysanthemum species
Consolida ajacis
Dianthus species
Eschscholzia californica
Gloriosa superba
Helianthus annuus
Hibiscus rosa-sinensis
Lavandula species
Lythrum species
Malva species
Monarda didyma
Oenothera biennis
Paeonia species
Papaver species
Passiflora species
Primula Polyanthus Group
Rosa species
Tagetes species
Tropaeolum majus
Viola species

HERBS FOR DRY SUN

Agave americana
Aloe vera
Artemisia species
Helichrysum italicum
Hyssopus officinalis
Lavandula species
Ocimum basilicum
Origanum species
Pelargonium species
Phlomis species
Rosmarinus officinalis
Salvia species
Santolina species
Sempervivum species
Thymus species
Verbascum species

HERBS FOR SHADE

Acanthus spinosus
Ajuga reptans
Alchemilla vulgaris
Allium schoenoprasm
Angelica archangelica
Aquilegia vulgaris
Buxus sempervirens
Digitalis species
Elaeagnus species
Ferns
Fragaria vesca
Galium odoratum
Gaultheria procumbens
Hamamelis virginiana
Hedera species
Ilex species
Impatiens balsamina
Lonicera species
Mahonia species
Mentha species
Petroselinum crispum
Primula vulgaris
Prunus laurocerasus
Pulmonaria officinalis
Sambucus nigra
Smyrnium olusatrum
Symphytum species
Vinca species
Viola species

Herb Garden Plant Key

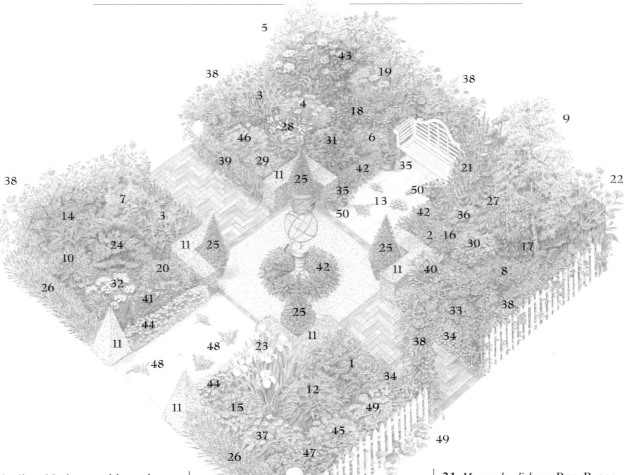

The herbs listed below, and keyed into the plan above, are featured in *My Classic Herb Garden* (pp.8–9). For plant descriptions, see pp.108–115.

1 *Achillea millefolium* YARROW
2 *Allium schoenoprasum* CHIVES
3 *Aloysia triphylla* LEMON VERBENA
4 *Anethum graveolens* DILL
5 *Angelica archangelica* ANGELICA
6 *Anthriscus cerefolium* CHERVIL
7 *Artemisia abrotanum*
  SOUTHERNWOOD
8 *Artemisia dracunculus* TARRAGON
9 *Betula pendula* SILVER BIRCH
10 *Borago officinalis* BORAGE
11 *Buxus sempervirens* BOXWOOD
12 *Calendula officinalis*
  POT MARIGOLD
13 *Chamaemelum nobile* CHAMOMILE
14 *Cichorium intybus* CHICORY
15 *Coriandrum sativum* CORIANDER

16 *Crocus sativus* SAFFRON
17 *Digitalis purpurea* FOXGLOVE
18 *Eruca vesicaria* subsp. *sativa*
  ARUGULA
19 *Foeniculum vulgare* FENNEL
20 *Galium odoratum*
  SWEET WOODRUFF
21 *Hyssopus officinalis* HYSSOP
22 *Inula helenium* ELECAMPANE
23 *Iris germanica* 'Florentina' ORRIS
24 *Juniperus communis* JUNIPER
25 *Laurus nobilis* BAY
26 *Lavandula angustifolia* LAVENDER
27 *Levisticum officinale* LOVAGE
28 *Lilium candidum* MADONNA LILY
29 *Melissa officinalis* LEMON BALM
30 *Mentha suaveolens* APPLE MINT

31 *Monarda didyma* BEE BALM
32 *Myrrhis odorata* SWEET CICELY
33 *Ocimum basilicum* BASIL
34 *Origanum vulgare* OREGANO
35 *Pelargonium capitatum* GERANIUM
36 *Petroselinum crispum* PARSLEY
37 *Phlomis fruticosa* JERUSALEM SAGE
38 *Rosa rugosa* 'Alba' RUGOSA ROSE
39 *Rosmarinus officinalis* ROSEMARY
40 *Rumex acetosa* SORREL
41 *Ruta graveolens* RUE
42 *Salvia officinalis* SAGE
43 *Sambucus nigra* ELDER
44 *Santolina chamaecyparissus*
  LAVENDER COTTON
45 *Tanacetum parthenium* FEVERFEW
46 *Tanacetum vulgare* TANSY
47 *Teucrium chamaedrys* GERMANDER
48 *Thymus serpyllum* 'Lemon Curd'
  THYME
49 *Tropaeolum majus* NASTURTIUM
50 *Viola odorata* SWEET VIOLET

PLANT INDEX

ACKNOWLEDGMENTS

AUTHOR'S ACKNOWLEDGMENTS

Special thanks to business partner Quentin Roake for his invaluable input and co-operation with the creation of this book.

Thanks also to the photographers, in particular Jonathan Buckley and Anne Hyde for their inspired location shots, and Stephen Hayward for the wonderful plant and flower studies filmed in his magnifcent studio.

I would like to acknowledge the help of my friends Mrs Franklin and Sarah Franklin, May Cristea, and Jenny and Richard Raworth as well as all the gardeners who allowed us to photograph in their gardens (see below).

My particular thanks to the Dorling Kindersley production team and especially Lesley Malkin, the project editor and Colin Walton, art editor, who were a truly inspirational team to work with. Also to E.E.S., John Austin and Terracottas of New Covent Garden Market, and Rosemary Titterington's Iden Croft Herbs who supplied many of the high quality plants, flowers, and pots for the book.

Last but not least, my warmest thanks to Rodney Engen for all his assistance and patience through the making of this book.

PUBLISHER'S ACKNOWLEDGMENTS

Thank you to Jo Weeks & Paula Hardy for editorial help; Robert Campbell for design help; Hilary Bird for compiling the index; Dr. Alan Hemsley for helping with plant identification; Larry Barlow for naming the chrysanthemums on pages 59 & 61; and Alan King & Vincent Charlton at Richmond Antiques for the loan of garden ornaments.

ILLUSTRATION CREDITS

Martine Collings 8, 116
Malcolm Hiller 10

PICTURE CREDITS

STUDIO PHOTOGRAPHY
Stephen Hayward
Matthew Ward

LOCATION PHOTOGRAPHY
Jonathan Buckley
Anne Hyde

ALL OTHER PHOTOGRAPHY BY

Deni Bown 109 tl, 111 tl; Lynne Brotchie / Garden Picture Library 98 bl; Brian Carter / Garden Picture Library 109 br, 110 tl, 110 tc, 112 br; Jill Cowley 106 br; Neil Fletcher 5 bl, 6 tr, 9, 108 tl, 108 bl, 109 bc, 111 br, 112 bl; Marijke Heuff / Garden Picture Library 113 tl; Michael Howes / Garden Picture Library 112 tr; Garden Matters 22 tr, 22 br, 107 bc; John Glover / Garden Picture Library 56 l, 63, 98 tr, 108 bc, 110 bc, 112 bc, 114 br; Derek Gould 96 tl, 96 bl; Jerry Harpur 108 br, 111 bl; Dave King 113 bl, 113 tr; Lamontagne / Garden Picture Library 8, 26 l, 109 bl; David Murray 107 br; Clive Nichols 22 l, 24 t; Gary Rogers / Garden Picture Library 92 t; Ron Sutherland / Garden Picture Library 107 tc; Nigel Temple / Garden Picture Library 48 l; Colin Walton 107 bl; and Didier Willery / Garden Picture Library 75 tl

GARDENS FEATURED

The photographers, author, and publishers express their gratitude for permission to photograph the following gardens:
The Anchorage, Kent (Mrs. Francis); Carwinion Garden, Mawnon Smith, Cornwall; Capel Manor, Hertfordshire; Chenies Manor, Buckinghamshire (Mrs. Mcleod Matthews); Clunton, Shropshire (Mrs. Price); Congham Hall Hotel, Norfolk; The Cottage Herbery, Tenbury Wells, Worcestershire; Doddinghton Hall, Lincolnshire; Margaret Easter, Hertfordshire; Elly Hill Herbs, Co. Durham; Endale, Shropshire (Mr. & Mrs. Johnston); The Geffrye Museum Herb Garden, London; Great Dixter, Sussex (Christopher Lloyd); Hall Place, Bexley; Hatfield House, Hertfordshire; Hawthorn Bank, Shropshire (Mrs. Buckley); Hexham Herbs, Northumberland (Susie White); Hill Farm Herbs, Northamptonshire; Holdenby House, Northamptonshire; Hollington Nurseries Berkshire (S & J Hopinson); Knebworth House, Hertfordshire; Iden Croft Herbs, Kent; Lambrooke Manor, Somerset; Lower Hall, Shropshire (Mr. & Mrs. Dumbell); Lower Severalls Herb Nursery, Somerset; Mallory Court Hotel, Warwickshire; Marle Place Kent (Mr. & Mrs. Williams); Merton Nurseries, Shropshire; The Old Rectory Berkshire; Radnor Cottage, Shropshire (Mr. & Mrs. Pitwood); RHS Garden, Wisley; Southview Nurseries, Hampshire; Sulgrave Manor, Northamptonshire; Toddington Manor, Bedfordshire; Wollerton Old Hall, Shropshire (John & Lesley Jenkins); Wyken Hall, Suffolk; Helen Yemm, London.